CHRISTIANITY ON THE OFFENSE

RESPONDING TO THE BELIEFS AND ASSUMPTIONS OF SPIRITUAL SEEKERS

by Dan Story

kregel
PUBLICATIONS

Grand Rapids, MI 49501

Christianity on the Offense: Responding to the Beliefs and Assumptions of Spiritual Seekers

Copyright © 1998 by Dan Story

Published in 1998 by Kregel Publications, a division of Kregel, Inc., P.O. Box 2607, Grand Rapids, MI 49501. Kregel Publications provides trusted, biblical publications for Christian growth and service. Your comments and suggestions are valued.

For more information about Kregel Publications, visit our web site at www.kregel.com.

Unless otherwise indicated, all Scripture quotations are from *The Holy Bible: New International Version* © 1978 by the International Bible Society. Used by permission of Zondervan Publishing House.

Cover design: PAZ Design Group
Book design: Frank Gutbrod

Library of Congress Cataloging-in-Publication Data
Story, Dan.
   Christianity on the offense: responding to the beliefs and assumptions of spiritual seekers / by Dan Story.
      p.   cm.
   Includes bibliographical references.
   1. Apologetics.   I. Title.
BT1102.S75   1998   239—dc21   98-10291
                                                 CIP

ISBN 0-8254-3676-1

Printed in the United States of America

1 2 3 / 03 02 01 00 99 98

To my children and grandchildren.

Behold, children are a gift of the LORD;
The fruit of the womb is a reward.
Like arrows in the hand of a warrior,
So are the children of one's youth.
How blessed is the man whose quiver is full of them.

Psalm 127:3–5

Contents

Part 1 "What is truth?"—*John 18:38*

Part 2 "You shall know the truth, and the truth shall make you free"—*John 8:32*

PART ONE

"What is truth?"
—John 18:38

An acquaintance recently gave me a computer printout containing a debate among two dozen employees at his workplace. The debate was carried on entirely through computers over a two-week period. The printout consisted of ninety-five comments and rebuttals—some of them rather lengthy—concerning the participants' views on religion, in particular Christianity. Judging by their remarks, the majority of the participants were unbelievers. The following are a few of their comments (most of them portions of fuller statements):

> *Unfortunately, most religions are hopelessly corrupted by ORGANIZED religion. Most organized religions . . . exist to further their own gains in power, influence, and money.*

> *Hypocrisy abounds in an organized religion [sic] structure. The basic concepts of a religion may allow an uneducated person to come to terms with the universe, to provide answers to "unanswerable" questions of existence.*

> *If you're a good person, then you should be fine with God.*

> *Religion is a man-made invention and therefore not subject to God's beliefs.*

As you are most likely aware, the teachings of Christ and the Buddha are more similar than not. The Dalai Lama, for one, suggests we celebrate the commonality of religious teachings rather than getting hung up on the differences.

Religion is the point in man's evolution where he begins to realize that there is a higher power [than himself] in the universe and then starts to worship it. He personalizes it and projects his own traits upon it.

Good and evil are extremely relative terms and are defined by man. Usually the results are the determining factor, but two different people will judge the results differently as well.

I know that this is a touchy subject, and nothing is harder to argue against than BELIEF, since it is not based on logic and facts.

I believe there is no god. If I'm wrong, it will be proven when and only when I die and meet god face-to-face. Until then, I will be no fool.

The person who gave me the printout is an engineer, and he prefaced the document by claiming that the people involved in the debate represent the "top five percent in intelligence."

Be this as it may, most of the comments were merely assumptions. Many of the ideas were logically inconsistent and subjective. They expressed personal opinions without objective verification. Comments about Christianity showed a high degree of biblical and theological illiteracy.

Please don't misunderstand me. I am not trying to belittle these people, nor am I attempting to dismiss their views as empty-headed. Rather, I want to point out that most of the arguments against Christianity—even those made by the "top five percent in intelligence"—are not all that sophisticated and can be dealt with by ordinary Christians with a little training. Certainly, there *are* sophisticated and technical arguments against our faith, and they must be dealt with by those qualified to do so. But it has been my experience that the majority of the arguments hurled against Christianity are relatively easy to respond to.

Most arguments against Christianity are based on faulty assumptions. They are poorly thought out. Few people seriously investigate Christian truth-claims and draw their own critical conclusions. Rather they simply pass on hearsay. For example, many people who claim that "the Bible is full of contradictions" usually admit that they have never read the Bible, nor can they point to a single contradiction in it. Their source of authority for this "truth-claim" is reduced to, "Well, *everyone* knows the Bible's full of contradictions!" Arguments such as these can be refuted by ordinary Christians who have been trained in apologetic techniques.

There are two ways to respond to arguments against Christianity, and the route taken will depend on the kind of objections raised. Some objections take the form of genuine questions: How do you know God exists? Doesn't evolution disprove creation? How do you know the Bible is true?

Such questions are obstacles to faith in Jesus Christ, and the goal is simply to remove them. The proper response is to provide a biblical answer supported by concrete, verifiable evidence. Hopefully, this will encourage the unbeliever to reconsider Christianity. This approach is "evidential" apologetics, and it has been a vital tool in evangelism since the beginnings of the Christian church.

However, as the computer debate illustrates, there are other types of objections raised by unbelievers. They are more philosophical and are part and parcel of broader, well-entrenched belief systems (worldviews). In the computer debate, the statements "If you're a good person, you should be fine with God," "Good and evil are extremely relative terms and are defined by man," and "Belief . . . is not based on logic and facts" represent beliefs that flow directly from modern, anti-Christian worldviews.

These kinds of objections require a different kind of response. They are neither simple misconceptions nor well-defined, clearly articulated questions.

The proper response to these kinds of objections is to deal with the *presuppositions* or assumptions on which they depend. If one's presuppositions are in error, all truth-claims flowing from them are equally false. A house built on a foundation of sand will crumble with the first rain regardless of how sound the rest of the house is built.

My earlier book, *Defending Your Faith: Reliable Answers for a New Generation of Seekers and Skeptics,* provides answers to the majority of the questions and misconceptions raised against Christianity. The purpose of this second book is to deal with the other variety of objections—those that are more philosophical, that arise directly from incorrect assumptions. This will be done in two parts.

In part 1, we will see *why* people think as they do: What role does one's worldview play in religious and ethical matters? Why are there so many contradicting worldviews, and how can we determine which one—if any— is true? Why does modern society expect us to accept all religions as equally valid? Are there rules for rational argumentation and discussion? What are they? Is there such a thing as absolute (final and perfect) truth? If there is, can it be discovered? Is there a standard outside of personal opinion by which religious truth can be judged? What is it? Can it prove that Christianity is the one true religion?

These and other topics are discussed in order to give a clear understanding of how unbelievers perceive reality and how religious truth can be established and tested.

In part 2, we will see *how* people think. We'll examine the major religious and secular worldviews that are seeking dominance in modern society—all with the expressed goal of usurping the authority and influence of Christianity. This section of the book will give insights into Christianity's major competitors, allowing the material in part 1 to be used effectively in apologetic evangelism.

Christians are confronted by dozens of religions and secular philosophies. We are told that *all* of them are equally legitimate—or equally fraudulent, depending on the critic. This book provides powerful evidence for the uniqueness of Christianity. Our faith is not a mindless religion. It has a firm foundation of objective facts that can be tested and verified.

If nothing else, this book will clearly demonstrate that Christianity, alone among the world's many religions and secular worldviews, is internally and externally consistent, rationally justifiable, objectively verifiable, and confirmed by human experience in a way that is completely in harmony with reality as almost all people understand it and live it out.

CHAPTER ONE

The World
We Live In

The United States in the late 1990s is not unlike the Roman Empire when Christianity exploded on the scene nearly two thousand years ago. Scholar David Wells described it this way:

> While religious pluralism may be a novel experience for us, it is putting us in touch with the world that surrounded the biblical authors probably more directly than any other. The pluralism and the paganism of Our Time were the common experiences of the prophets and apostles. In Mesopotamia, there were thousands of gods and goddesses, many of which were known to the Israelites—indeed, sometimes known too well. In Christ's time, there were hundreds of sects of one kind or another along the Mediterranean rim. Moreover, there was the official Roman religion that blended politics and religion through a deification of the Caesars, in due course becoming a formidable enemy to Christian faith. And there was Greek philosophy as well, much of it also functioning as a set of competing religions. Pluralism was the stuff of everyday life in biblical times.[1]

This religious diversity was characterized by tolerance. In spite of their differences, the numerous religions more or less accepted one another. It was generally agreed that all religions possessed a measure of intrinsic value. Conflict was rare.[2]

Of course then, as now, Christians refused to acknowledge the merits of other religions and sought to convert the pagans to Christianity.[3] This eventually contributed to widespread persecution, which continued until the time of Constantine in the early fourth century. Christianity later became the state religion of Rome and the dominant worldview in Western culture. Meanwhile, pagan religions moved off center stage and into the wings.

Modern Christianity competes with a similar smorgasbord of religious ideologies and practices. The only difference between the Roman world and today is that the menu has changed somewhat. Christianity in the United States coexists "with Mormonism, . . . Buddhism, Islam, and much more—a total of about 1200 separate religious bodies."[4]

In addition to competing with twelve hundred religions, Christianity also faces a variety of atheistic ideologies, all of which contribute to the philosophical milieu of modern secular humanism.

Secular Humanism

Secular humanists believe that all religions were created by people. They consider people, rather than God, supreme in the universe. Their worldview seeks to push religious thought and life to the outer perimeter of human concerns—if not eliminate them altogether.

Secular humanism has usurped Christianity as the guiding social force in Western culture. It determines what is true in the areas of ethics, religious practices, social behavior, and modern science and psychology. Contributing secular humanist philosophies include the following.

Evolution. The belief that life came into existence accidentally through natural, random processes over immense periods of time without the aid of a Higher Being. There is no God.

Materialism. The belief that all of reality is material (matter). Nothing spiritual or nonmaterial exists. Immortal souls or spirits do not exist; no mind exists independent of the brain.[5] Even our thoughts can be reduced to chemical and neurological processes. There is no God.

Naturalism. This philosophy asserts that the universe is all there is and ever was and that all within it operate according to eternal, universal, unchanging natural laws. All of reality can be understood in terms of natural processes. There are no supernatural beings or supernatural events such as miracles and answered prayer. There is no God.

Postmodernism. The traditional form of secular humanism is rapidly evolving—especially in academia—into a new worldview that rejects objective truth and reason. In postmodernism, absolute truth is non-existent. "Truth" is *subjective* in that it is directly related to one's cultural beliefs and experiences. *Pluralism* and *relativism* are the foundational presuppositions of postmodernism.

Tolerance Untolerated

In light of the multitude of religions and philosophies permeating modern society, historians often refer to today's world as "pluralistic," "relativistic," and "global." Civilization is comprised of many worldviews, all of which are considered to represent truth (pluralism). Moreover, religious and ethical beliefs are dependent upon the circumstances that define them. Truth flows from one's personal beliefs or from one's culture and can vary under different situations (relativism).

Furthermore, individual worldviews do not exist in isolation. They can and do have great influence on each other, interacting and assimilating the beliefs and practices of numerous peoples, cultures, and religions throughout the world (globalism).

Pluralism is extremely dangerous to Christianity because it is such a powerful force undermining the discovery of religious truth.[6] Pluralism not only extends the hand of fellowship to hundreds of religions, but it also congratulates them for being expressions of religious truth. All religions are equally valid.

Proponents of religious pluralism believe that *all* religions possess a common core of beliefs and experiences. All religions more or less talk about the same "God." Alister McGrath explained it this way:

> This naturally leads to the idea that dialogue between religions can lead to an enhancement of truth, in that the limited perspectives of one religion can be complemented by the differing perspectives of another. As all religions are held to relate to the same reality, dialogue thus constitutes a privileged mode of access to truth.[7]

Religious pluralism loudly condemns any form of "narrow-minded bigotry" that seeks to elevate one religion as supreme over any other. Professor D. A. Carson explained it with these words:

> In the religious field, this means that few people will be offended by the multiplying new religions. No matter how wacky, no matter how flimsy their intellectual credentials, no matter how subjective and uncontrolled, no matter how blatantly self-centered, no matter how obviously their gods

have been manufactured to foster human self-promotion, the media will treat them with fascination and even a degree of respect. But if any religion claims that in some measure other religions are wrong, a line has been crossed and resentment is immediately stirred up: pluralism . . . has been challenged. Exclusiveness is the one religious idea that cannot be tolerated.[8]

The significance of this in the religious marketplace cannot be overstated. Carson continued:

Pluralism has managed to set in place certain "rules" for playing the game of religion—rules that transcend any single religion. These rules are judged to be axiomatic. They include the following: religiously based exclusive claims must be false; what is old or traditional in religion is suspect and should probably be superseded; "sin" is a concept steeped in intolerance. The list could easily be expanded.[9]

There is obvious irony here. One would expect a pluralistic, relativistic, and global world to have an open forum for discussing and evaluating religious truth. Nothing is further from the truth. If any cardinal doctrine characterizes religious pluralism, it is an *unwillingness* to critically discuss and compare religious beliefs. This is especially true if the purpose is to discover truth, that is to determine which religion, if any, can sustain its truth-claims. Again, Carson made a valuable comment:

Those who are committed to the proposition that all views are equally valid have eliminated the possibility that one or more of those opinions has a special claim to being true or valid. They have foreclosed on open-mindedness in the same breath by which they extol the virtues of open-mindedness; they are dogmatic about pluralism. . . .

Both the irony and the tragedy of this fierce intolerance stem from the fact that it is done in the name of tolerance. It is not "liberal education" in the best sense; it is not pluralism in the best sense. It is fundamentalistic dogmatism in the worse sense. . . .

. . . Small wonder, then, that Stanley S. Harakas can affirm that the prevailing world view in America is not pluralistic . . . but atomistic and anti-religious.[10]

In sum, religious pluralism strives mightily to prevent one from ever discovering absolute truth—what is really true as opposed to what is personal opinion or mere belief. It does this under the guise of tolerance and political correctness. If religious truth is to be found at all, it will not come from the religious pluralism that characterizes the modern scene.

Religions Resurrected

In the last few decades, religious practices that vanished as dominant beliefs centuries ago have reemerged. This phenomenon is paradoxical, considering the modern world's steady shift toward secular humanism. It illustrates the fact that people seek to maintain a religious relevance to their lives. This is done in spite of an evolving secular worldview that is rapidly moving Westerners away from their Christian roots. The modern world may be rejecting Christianity, but it still clings tenaciously to humanity's innate need to come to terms with spiritual realities.

Both the Bible and secular studies attest to the fact that people everywhere and in every culture and period of history instinctively recognize the existence of God.[11] They seek to understand Him, and they seek to relate to Him. True atheism is an anomaly. It is a deviation from the norm. Even thoroughly secularized people seek after God. Let me cite two examples of these resurrected religious worldviews.

Polytheism Proliferated

Polytheism is an ancient religious practice that believes in the existence of numerous personal gods and goddesses. These beings are finite, in the sense that they arose from sexual relationships or from the life forces of nature itself, and generally they rule over specific domains. For example, Poseidon (Neptune) rules the sea, Hades (Pluto) rules the underworld, while Zeus (Jupiter) is the "Lord of the Sky, the Rain-god and the Cloud-gatherer, who wielded the awful thunderbolt."[12]

Polytheism began to fade as a dominant religious force in Western culture with the breakdown of the Greek and Roman Empires. Centuries later, however, it is making new inroads into Western culture and is becoming an acceptable religious worldview. Geisler and Watkins made this report:

> Polytheism has a long history in both the West and the East. Many Eastern religions and philosophies have been and still are polytheistic. Among these are some forms of Hinduism, Confucianism, Shinto, Taoism, and Jainism. In the West, the belief in many gods appears in several of the ancient Greek writers, like Hesiod and Homer (eighth

century B.C.), and throughout the ancient culture of the Roman Empire. There are several distinct manifestations of polytheism in contemporary Western society, including Mormonism, the Divine Light Mission, Scientology, the Unification Church. . . . In addition, there are the occult forms of polytheism, including the UFO religions and the extraterrestrial types.[13]

To this list can be added a growing interest in witchcraft and ancient pagan religions and cults.

Why are polytheistic religions being resurrected? Because, as Geisler and Watkins put it, they need "to help man deal with his pluralistic experience. . . . because life and meaning are pluralistic, man must be polytheistic in order to think and speak about it."[14] In a society that accepts numerous *contradicting* beliefs as truth, polytheism is a religion that fits. It endorses the pluralistic worldview prevalent today. People today believe in "God" but see Him differently in His essential nature (pluralism). Polytheism promotes a form of religious syncretism that people think is necessary to avoid religious confrontation and bigotry.

Deism Dispersed

The second example of a resurrected worldview is Deism. This religious worldview flourished in the United States and Europe from the late seventeenth century through the eighteenth century, but it more or less vanished in the nineteenth century. Like Christians, Deists believed in an infinite, personal God who created the world and the natural laws that sustain it. Deists taught, however, that after this initial creative act, God withdrew to allow the universe to operate unaided by further divine interference. Thus supernatural actions, such as miracles, never occur. Revelation is limited to "general revelation," and all that can be known about God and morality can be discovered through nature and human reasoning.

Today, although largely unrecognized, a form of *neo-deism* is prevalent throughout the West. Its adherents are people who claim to be Christian, who still profess to believe in the God of Scripture, and who identify culturally with Christianity, but these people live lives as if God does not exist. George Barna's annual survey of religious views in America confirms this:

> In studying the spiritual perspectives of Americans, confusing or contradictory findings sometimes emerge. Although millions of Americans can describe or affirm various religious beliefs, they do not take these perspec-

tives so seriously as to integrate them into the fabric of their lives. . . . The average American . . . is neither a deep theological thinker nor worries about the importance of developing life-shaping religious convictions. . . . Large majorities of people now claim that the Bible and religion are very important in their lives, but there is little evidence that this change in attitude has influenced the way they live.[15]

Neo-deists are individuals who do not want to reject the Christian idea of a personal God in favor of a pagan or pantheistic view of God (as in polytheism and the New Age), but they want to preserve their sovereignty and independence from God. They do not outright reject God, but neither do they know Him or follow Him. They think of God as somehow remotely involved in human affairs but not actively so. They are more secular than Christian. The Bible, understandably, condemns this kind of "Christianity" in Titus 1:16 and elsewhere.

The Problem at Hand

In light of the pluralistic world in which we live, it is no wonder that skeptics and critics are cynical when Christians claim that they alone possess religious truth. In a pluralistic society that accepts all worldviews, such a claim sounds intellectually arrogant and theologically naive.

Christians, however, are not alone in making this claim. Although our society is largely pluralistic and although some religions accept the view that God is revealed in all religions, *many* religions claim to possess the final and absolute word in the area of religious truth. Even religions that do not openly claim such knowledge still make absolute statements about religious truth. To say that all religions are divine expressions of truth is an absolute statement about religious truth.

Most people—including many Christians—are so conditioned by pluralism that they fail to recognize the blatant and irreconcilable contradictions that exist among the world's many religions and philosophies. Even when they do, our pluralistic society expects them to keep quiet about it. The person who criticizes another person's beliefs—whether religious, moral, sexual, or otherwise—is ridiculed as intolerant and bigoted. The only exception, of course, is when the person being criticized is a Christian. It is always open season on Christians, and it's perfectly acceptable to criticize "narrow-minded fundamentalists." But here's the problem. When contradicting views claim to be ultimate truth, only one view can logically be true.

Consider the nature of God. It is fundamental to a religion's other doctrines. Salvation, for example, is directly tied in to a religion's view of God and how He relates to people. Portraying the true nature of God is critical if a religion is to represent absolute truth in the area of salvation. The same is true for any other doctrine. The nature of God as portrayed in any religion will necessarily reflect that religion's concept of sin, evil, morality, and human nature.

But all major religions disagree on the nature of God. Pantheists, for example, claim that God is an impersonal, all-encompassing "It" that permeates the universe. For a pantheist, God and nature are one and the same.

Polytheists believe in many personal gods and goddesses. Each god is identified with some aspect of life or part of the created universe.

Christianity teaches that there is only one God. Unlike pantheism, Christianity teaches that God is personal. He is distinct from creation by virtue of being the Creator.

If logic has any meaning at all, it is impossible for all such contradictory views of God to be true. Only one view can reveal the true nature of God.

It's like mathematics. There can only be one correct answer to any equation. Four plus four is eight. Seven is almost eight, but it still isn't eight. It doesn't matter how close to the number eight you may be: any other answer is wrong. Likewise if two different religions claim that their view of God is the only correct view, then one or both groups are not worshiping the true God. Both religions may be wrong in their view of God, but they cannot both be right.

At first blush, polytheism may appear to solve this dilemma because it accepts all gods. But this solution won't hold up to closer scrutiny. Why? Both Christianity and pantheism reject a multiplicity of gods, so we are back to the same dilemma.[16] If Christianity or pantheism reveal the true nature of God, then polytheism must be incorrect. In either case, only one of the three—or none—can ultimately portray religious truth.

A Matter of Life and Death

If you are a believer in religious pluralism, you may be thinking, So what! Yet these issues are important. If logically only one religion can depict the true nature of God, then only that religion can reveal God's plan of salvation.

Pluralism removes the urgency to search for religious truth because it accepts all religions as "paths to the same mountain top" (i.e., to God and salvation). But this is an impossibility. All paths but one lead *away* from God. It is critical to understand this so that we will be motivated to seek after the true God. Unless He is found, we will never discover religious truth, we will never discover the true path to salvation, and we will never discover how to live a more abundant life in the here and now. Everyone's eternal destiny rests on the outcome of this quest.

The challenge to Christian evangelists is to learn how to convince unbelievers of this logically necessary truth: Only one religion can be true; all others must be frauds. Of course, there is a second problem facing evangelists. If we convince unbelievers that only one religion can reveal spiritual truth, how do we convince them that Christianity is that religion?

We will discover the answer to this question by exploring the nature of truth, how it is determined, and how it can be confirmed. This will be the focus of the remaining chapters of part 1.

CHAPTER TWO

Firming the Foundation of Truth

There is no greater threat facing the true Church of Christ at this moment than the irrationalism that now controls our entire church. Communism, guilty of tens of millions of murders, including those of millions of Christians, is to be feared, but not nearly so much as the idea that we do not and cannot know truth. Hedonism, the popular philosophy of America, is not to be feared so much as the belief that logic—that "mere human logic," to use the religious irrationalists' own phrase—is futile. The attack on truth, on revelation, on the intellect, and on logic are renewed daily. But note well: The misologists—the haters of logic—use logic to demonstrate the futility of using logic. The anti-intellectuals construct intricate intellectual arguments to prove the insufficiency of the intellect.[1]

We do well to heed this warning from Gordon H. Clark about irrationalism. Anybody can claim anything, but claiming doesn't make it true. Anybody can believe anything, but believing doesn't make it true. One can sincerely believe in something and be sincerely wrong. There has to be some criteria for determining religious truth if religious truth is to be known at all.[2]

There are such criteria, and we will spend considerable time examining them in the following chapters. But first there are two fundamental concepts that must be understood in order for this criteria to be meaningful. Together, they form the basis of all truth and knowledge.

Truth Corresponds to Reality

Truth is a fact that, by its very nature, is immutable—it *cannot* change. As James Sire put it, truth is "propositional: a statement is true if what it says is so is so, or if what it says is not so is not so."[3] This means that whatever is true must be in agreement with and conform to reality. What is reality? It's what's real—"the way things really are."[4] It is what exists independent of people's personal opinions and beliefs. Let me illustrate this.

Let's say I misplaced my dictionary. I think it's on my desk (what I believe is truth), but actually it's on the kitchen table (reality). So the truth of the situation is that the dictionary is on the table independent of my belief that it's on the desk. Thus, truth (the location of my dictionary) corresponds to reality (where it actually is). It doesn't matter what I believe; it's a matter of what is true.

The "correspondence theory of truth" holds that what one *thinks* is true *is true* when it matches what is real. We possess true knowledge about something when what we think is true agrees with what exists outside our minds. If I think my dictionary is on my desk and it *is* on my desk, then what I hold to be true matches reality—my knowledge of the location of my dictionary corresponds to reality.

Truth, then, must correspond to reality. The alternative is that actual truth is non-existent. What people perceive as truth would depend upon their personal feelings or their particular worldview. In either case, whatever seems to be true relative to one's particular beliefs or opinions becomes truth, and whatever does not fit with one's beliefs is non-truth.

Obviously, if truth is bound to one's private beliefs, it may differ from person to person or from culture to culture. This means that universal and unchanging truth is impossible to discover because it does not exist. This in turn means that statements of universal fact are also nonexistent and ultimate reality is unknowable. In short, all truth, if it exists, must correspond to reality. You may find comfort in knowing that most of science operates according to the correspondence theory of truth.[5]

Truth Depends on First Principles

There is a second concept that needs to be understood before we examine criteria for determining truth. There exist universal "first principles" (or "universal givens," or "fundamental laws of human belief") which govern how *all* people in *every* culture throughout *all* of history reason. (Some religions and philosophies deny the existence of these universal principles, but they live and behave as if these principles *do* exist.)

Examples include such concepts as I exist, other people exist, what I see exists, the past existed, there is a real, material world outside my mind, what I hear are real sounds, and the laws of nature are real and will endure. Also included are the "laws of logic," which we will look at more closely in a moment.

It is because of these first principles that we can determine that truth *does* correspond to reality and that it is universally applicable. These principles are foundational to all thought and knowledge. They need no confirmation because they are necessarily true—that is, they are undeniable and self-evident. They must exist. Their veracity rests on their own premises rather than on external evidences—although they are certainly confirmed by our everyday experiences. If they needed any proof, they would not be first principles. They stand alone.

Here is an analogy that may help you to see this clearly. Everything in the universe is contingent; it depends on something else for its existence. A tree depends on minerals, water, and sunshine. Canyons depend on erosion. Living things depend on other living things from which they are born. This implies that there must be a first cause—something from which all else springs. Christians claim that this first cause, on which the entire universe rests and has it being, is God. He is, if you will, the first principle. While everything has a cause for its existence, God is self-existing. He had no cause. He has no justification for His existence because He always existed and is the source of everything else.

In like manner, universal first principles are necessarily self-existing and self-justifying. They are the "first cause" of all contingent thought and knowledge. Just as God is the ultimate source of the universe, so are self-evident first principles the foundation of all truth-claims. No truth can violate them because all truth depends upon them. If a truth-claim violates these first principles, by definition it is false.

Actually, if you think about it, I am not saying anything remarkable or anything you do not already know. We instinctively use these first principles all the time without realizing it. We just take them for granted. They are the necessary principles that govern all human reasoning and communication, and without them we would be unable not only to discern truth but also even to think.

The Laws of Logic

The most fundamental of these first principles are the laws of logic, in particular the "law of non-contradiction." It states that something cannot be two different things at the same time and in the same sense ("A" cannot be both "A" and "non-A" at the same time and in the same relationship). For example, it can't be both raining and sunny outside at the same time in the same spot. My dog can't be both sleeping under a shrub and chewing a sprinkler head on the lawn at the same time. If it were possible for contradictions to mutually exist, there would be no difference between true and false, black and white, up or down, and so on. Truth would be impossible to discuss, and facts would forever elude us.

The law of non-contradiction is particularly important in determining religious truth. Simply put, it prevents two contradicting religions from both being true. I will illustrate this in just a moment.

Other foundational laws of logic include the "law of identity" ("A" is "A"—my dog is a dog), the law of excluded middle (either "A" or "non-A"—if I declare I'm petting my dog, I'm either doing it or not), and the law of rational inference (assuming my premises are correct, I can derive logical or true conclusions).[6]

Besides these basic laws of logic, there are also self-evident propositions (statements of truth) that are equally foundational to all thought and knowledge. (These propositions are also first principles.) They include: something can be known, opposites cannot both be true, everything cannot be false, something exists, nothing cannot produce something, everything that comes to be is caused, as well as self-defining tautologies such as all husbands are married and all triangles have three sides.[7]

Without these universal laws of logic, it would be impossible to make heads or tails out of the world, let alone discover truth. To deny them would be to sacrifice a rational world and to prevent any meaningful communication. Indeed, it is because of these universal laws of logic that people from different cultures and with different languages can communicate with one another and come to an agreement on what constitutes truth and reality— religious and otherwise.

For Example

Let's look at the person who rejects the correspondence theory of truth and claims that reality is relative to one's worldview.

Christian Scientists fall into this category. Their religious worldview teaches that sickness and pain are an illusion; they do not exist. But this belief is valid only by rejecting the fact that truth corresponds to reality. Is their belief borne out in practice? Hardly!

When Christian Scientists fall and break an arm, they feel pain. They may claim the pain is an illusion, but they go to a doctor anyway. Even if the broken arm *is* an illusion, the illusion itself is so real that it hurts. There is no difference between illusion or reality so far as the reactions to the broken arm are concerned.

If we live in a world where illusion is seen and treated as reality, what is the point in calling it an illusion? The claim that the broken arm is an illusion may be consistent with the Christian Scientists' worldview, but it is not consistent with reality (what is real) as people universally live it out. That the arm is broken is more real than the illusion that it is not.

Admitting pain and going to a doctor invalidates the Christian Scientists' worldview because it is logically inconsistent with how they interface with reality. The reality of their pain and their reaction of going to the doctor *corresponds* to the *truth* that the broken arm is not an illusion.[8]

You see, it is not a matter of what is real to me may not be real to you. It is a matter of what really is real. I may "sincerely believe" it's not raining outside, but if I go outside and it *is* raining, I'll get wet in spite of my beliefs.

As an example of how the laws of logic can be violated, let's return to the subject of pluralism. Pluralism assumes that all religions reflect divine truth in spite of their obvious contradictions. Such a claim flies in the face of the operating laws of logic by which people live and think. It disputes the very means by which we are able to understand reality in all areas of human life. People who expect us to accept religious pluralism are asking us to reject the law of non-contradiction. They are asking us to believe the absurd.

For example, it is logically impossible for contradicting religions to all represent truth. The true nature of God is either monotheistic, pantheistic, or something else. God cannot be both monotheistic and pantheistic. Likewise, the resurrection of Jesus. The New Testament clearly teaches that Jesus rose from the grave. The Koran denies it. Both cannot be right.

Here is one more example. Many Eastern religions and their New Age clones tell us that to see truth we must get "beyond" logic. This is utter nonsense. Whatever getting beyond logic entails, it would require logical thinking to accomplish it. Thus the idea of "getting beyond logic" is a self-destroying proposition. As Mark Hanna put it, "There is no way to escape the horns of this dilemma. The employment of logic in the attempt to refute logic is an implicit acknowledgment of the certainty and absoluteness of logic."[9]

To move beyond logic is to move into rational chaos and a total breakdown of our ability to understand and reason. To move beyond logic would not lead to truth but would make truth impossible to discover.

Summary
God has placed in human beings, by virtue of being created in His image, the ability to reason and to think logically. This is what separates humanity

from the beasts. God created a rational world that subscribes to the laws of logic and other first principles. When we are encouraged to accept religious beliefs that fly in the face of these laws and self-evident truths, doubts occur. And rightly they should!

If we are to proceed any further in our search for religious truth, we must agree that truth corresponds to reality and that it never violates universal, absolute principles of logic. Only by strictly adhering to these laws can we determine truth from error among conflicting religious worldviews. If you reject these laws, you may as well close this book right now (as well as your mind) because truth will forever elude you.

CHAPTER THREE

Is Truth Relatively True or Absolutely True?

Have you ever heard comments like these?

Homosexuality? It's just another lifestyle. It's not for me, of course, but if someone wants that kind of relationship, why shouldn't he? It's a free country, isn't it?

Pornography? I think it's terrible. But we can't close down the peep shows and adult bookstores just because it's smut. We have to protect everyone's constitutional right of free speech.

Abortion? I don't agree with it personally, but a woman has a right to do whatever she wants with her own body.

Christians? They're so narrow-minded and exclusive. Why should they have a monopoly on God? God can reveal Himself in any religion. I believe that all religions are paths to the same mountain top.

These comments have one thing in common. They reflect an increasingly popular belief in Western culture, especially in the area of ethics and religion. It is the claim that truth is relative; it flows from individual beliefs, cultural worldviews, or circumstances rather than from an objective standard (such as God) that exists beyond human subjectivity (beyond personal opinion). In such a system, if beliefs, worldviews, and circumstances vary depending on geography and period of history, then truth must vary as well because it depends on these entities to give it meaning. Truth, then, is not universal and unchanging. Rather it is enslaved to a variety of interpretations.

The philosophy of relativism springs from two foundational presuppositions (assumptions).[1] First, what was once true may not be true anymore. Adultery was immoral in the 1950s but may not be in the 1990s. Homosexuality was a sin in the past but is an acceptable lifestyle today. Second, what is true for me may not be true for you. Abortion may be evil to me but not to you. God may reveal Himself to me in Christianity, but He may reveal Himself to you in Hinduism.

Relativism is widely accepted because these two presuppositions are part and parcel of modern pluralism. Take, for example, religious pluralism—the belief that all religions reflect truth. Religious pluralism can only be sustained if truth is relative. Why? Because the world's major religions contradict one another in their essential doctrines. Only the claim that truth is relative prevents religious pluralism from crumbling.

If religious relativism is true, it follows that ethical relativism is also true. Aren't ethics generally a product of religion? Thus, just as there are no religious absolutes, there are no moral absolutes. Moral truths change with time and circumstances and are determined by culture or personal opinion, not God.

The philosophy of relativism teaches that absolute truth, truth that is applicable to all people at all times, is non-existent. Over the past few decades, this philosophy has become widely accepted and represents one of the most significant worldview changes in modern Western society. More and more people believe that truth and ethical behavior are neither determined by God nor revealed as absolute principles through the Judeo-Christian religion. Rather they are a result of personal beliefs and experiences as interpreted by one's culture.

A recent survey by the Barna Research Group asked the question, Is there absolute truth? The survey revealed that the majority of American adults believe that there is no such thing as absolute truth and that different people can define truth in contradictory ways and all be correct. Says George Barna:

> Last year's study [1991] discovered that the vast majority of Americans do not believe in absolute truth. If you combine that insight with the prevailing perceptions about sin, you might conclude that although Americans believe in

the idea of sin, they reject the notion of an absolute definition of sin. Thus, an act that is a sin in my eyes may not be
something you would consider sinful. To most adults, this
conflict in perspective is perfectly permissible. When all
truth is deemed relative, so is the evaluation of our actions.[2]

This surprising (and alarming) fact becomes paradoxical when we consider that 88 percent of American adults say they are Christians, and that
two-thirds of the nation's adults claim to have made a personal commitment to Jesus Christ.[3] Add this to the fact that 56 percent of all adults
"strongly" agree that the Bible is the "written Word of God and is totally
accurate in all that it teaches" (and another 18 percent agree with this statement "somewhat"[4]), and you are forced to conclude that most Americans
do not understand what being a Christian is. They fail to recognize that
biblical truth-claims are absolute statements about reality and not open to
personal opinion. Relativism has infiltrated their thinking.

Relativism and Christianity Are Mutually Exclusive

Relativism is diametrically opposed to the clear teachings of Scripture.
The Bible specifically states that God is the sovereign, absolute authority
in the universe (1 Sam. 2:6; Pss. 24:1; 50:10; 135:6). It logically follows
that all truth and moral principles revealed in Scripture (God's recorded
revelation) are likewise absolute. Accordingly in the Christian worldview,
truth and ethics are unchanging, universal, and applicable to all cultures
regardless of circumstances or period of history (Rom. 2:13; Exod. 20).
This means that what is true in the past is true today, and what is true for
me is true for you. This also means that ethics are prescriptive—they tell
us how we *should* act (whether we do so or not) because ethics represent
truth *independent* of personal or cultural opinion.

In the Christian worldview, ultimate reality is God. Truth is universal
and unchanging because God is universal (Deut. 33:27; Isa. 57:15; Rev.
4:10) and unchanging (1 Sam. 15:29; Mal. 3:6; Heb. 6:17). Adultery and
homosexuality are just as wrong in the 1990s as they were in the 1950s.
Abortion is wrong for everyone. People change, worldviews change—either
moving toward or away from truth—but truth itself is unchanging because
it corresponds to ultimate reality: God.

Why Relativism Fails

The case against relativism is not just a matter of philosophical differences between relativists and Christians. There are other issues to con-

sider. Let's look at a few other ways in which relativism fails to correspond to reality.

Relativism is immoral. Followed to its logical conclusion, relativism will ultimately lead to moral anarchy and the disintegration of civilization. Think about this for a moment. If we were free to determine our own standard of morality (moral truth), laws would be meaningless and human rights could not exist.

Laws are standards that govern behavior—more accurately, standards that restrict behavior. Laws are byproducts of absolutism. They apply to everyone equally and are not open to private interpretation. They tell people how to act whether they want to or not.

Relativism, on the other hand, if it is consistent and true to itself, teaches that we determine our own ethical behavior. Thus law, in the sense of absolute standards for conduct, and relativism are mutually exclusive. They are opposite concepts. There can be no absolute law in a relative society where individuals, or even whole cultures, determine their own moral truth and ethical conduct.

What does this mean? In a society practicing relativism, if someone disagrees with a particular law, they would be free to ignore it. It means that when people with opposing views collide, the physically or politically stronger parties are free to impose their opinions on the weaker. "You can believe what you want, but you'll do things my way because I'm tougher than you!" For instance, if I need a car, I'll just steal yours. Stealing is not a sin to me, as long as I'm doing the stealing. But you'd better not try to steal my car because if you steal my car, it _is_ a sin.

In short, if a society's moral structure is based on a relativism that flows from individual opinion—as some people promote—"survival of the fittest" ultimately determines ethical behavior and morality. Laws are philosophically defined out of existence.

One may argue that in reality it does not work that way. Relativism does not leave individuals free to act as they choose. Rather relativism plays itself out on a cultural level. In other words, society, rather than individuals, sets the standards, and people obey the "laws of the land" as dictated by that culture. But each culture is free to set its own standards—thus relativism still works.

Sorry, no cigar.

Relativism, carried to its logical conclusion, leads to moral anarchy on a broad, cultural scale just as readily is it does on an individual scale. This is especially evident in the modern world where cultures bump up against one another. In a relativistic world, international peace is impossible.

If standards of right and wrong were culturally controlled, one nation could never condemn the actions of another nation.

Iraq's invasion of Kuwait a few years ago would have been perfectly acceptable because the Iraqis agreed it was correct behavior. It wouldn't have mattered what Kuwait or the rest of the world believed.

Likewise, one nation could never condemn the actions that another nation takes *even against its own people.* The systematic slaughter of six million Jews during the Holocaust of World War II would have been permissible because it was not "against the law" in Nazi Germany. The Nazis believed the Jews were vermin to be exterminated.

I am sure you see my point. In the real world, no nation can live consistently with the philosophy of relative ethics and still maintain a civilized society. Someone outside and above corporate humanity and personal preference (i.e., God) must be the source of ethics and must motivate people to be obedient to those ethics. Without such a moral absolute, ethics become relative and subject to human greed and capriciousness.

Relativism is illogical. A second way in which relativism fails to correspond to reality is that it flies in the face of the laws of logic. For example, the law of non-contradiction is foundational to all rational thought and communication. All truth depends on this necessary first principle. But relativism violates the law of non-contradiction. Like pluralism as a whole, it takes blatantly contradictory truth-claims and states that both are correct. This is logically impossible. Christianity and pantheism cannot both reveal the true nature of God because their respective Gods are conspicuously different. Indeed, they are mutually exclusive. Likewise, if a man justifies adultery and his wife condemns it as sin, both opinions can't be correct. It's either sin or it's acceptable behavior: it can't be both at the same time. Logically, relativism does not make sense.

Relativism is inconsistent. No one lives the philosophy of relativism consistently. In daily life, all people live and behave according to the same understanding of what constitutes reality. One of the clearest examples of this is in the area of ethical behavior.

Comparative studies in anthropology, sociology, and religion have revealed a universal, worldwide moral code governing the behavior of all peoples, regardless of their culture, religion, or the period of history in which they existed. Not only Western culture, but also Eastern societies of Hindus, Buddhists, and Egyptians have had a similar concept of right and wrong. Even primitive cultures have exhibited this universal awareness of what is evil. This innate sense of right and wrong helps people everywhere judge the injustice of others and themselves. (This doesn't sound like relativism, does it?)

The generic moral code is manifested in worldwide prohibitions against murder, stealing, lying, rape, and cheating.[5] A culture may differ on how these ethical mandates are played out, but the prohibitions themselves are universal. As Francis Beckwith pointed out, "It does not follow from different practices that people have different values."[6]

For example, adultery may be acceptable in some societies, but no society allows a man to just take any woman he wants. Stealing may not be a sin if carried out against another tribe, but you do not steal from your neighbor. Lying may be acceptable in certain situations. Killing may be permitted in warfare. But all people agree that it is wrong to steal from, lie to, or murder just anyone. The concepts of stealing, lying, and killing are universally recognized as evil, and such acts are strictly controlled in every culture. People may claim ethics are relative, but all people enforce a universal moral code.

Now let's look at this same principle more specifically. Do individual people who tout relativism live consistently with it? The answer is no.

Many Americans believe that truth is relative and that people should be free to behave pretty much as they believe. However, people who preach relativism practice absolutism. For example, if someone steals a car, the victims (relativists) immediately recognize that theft as a sin and call the police. If a man commits adultery, his wife experiences profound hurt even if she believes that ethics are relative. These reactions and feelings demonstrate that relativism is inconsistent with the real world. Relativists simply do not practice what they preach.

If ethics were relative, there would be no moral or philosophical grounds for condemning the thief who thinks stealing a car is acceptable or for being upset when one's spouse commits adultery. As Beckwith wrote, "In order to remain consistent the ethical relativist cannot criticize intolerable moral practices, believe in real moral progress, or acknowledge the existence of real moral reformers. For these three forms of moral judgment presupposes the existence of real transcultural nonrelative objective values" [i.e., the kind of absolute moral standards we receive from God].[7]

By appealing to the police, relativists admit to a universal code of behavior that applies to *both* them and the thief (remember, laws point to absolutism, not relativism). By feeling pain, the woman is acknowledging that adultery is wrong even if she accepts moral relativity. In both cases, they are admitting to a standard of right and wrong that applies to other people. This is absolutism.

People talk the talk of relativism but live the life of absolutism. Relativism is a philosophy, a worldview. To be valid, it must work in any and all situations. Otherwise it cannot represent truth. You can't pick and choose where relativism applies and where is doesn't. You either live with it or reject it. If you think stealing and adultery are wrong for all people, you are an absolutist.

Relativism is self-destructive. The fourth reason relativism fails to correspond to reality is because it is self-destructive. It denies itself. Remember, truth must correspond to reality, the actual state of things. Relativism, however, means that something is dependent upon something else to give it meaning. But if something is dependent upon something else to give it meaning, it cannot be true standing alone. This means that relativism cannot make absolute statements about reality (i.e., truth) because, standing alone, it does not reflect the actual state of the matter.

This may sound confusing, so let me try to illustrate what I'm saying. If some people say that adultery is wrong in some situations but not in others, they are saying that adultery is relative to (determined by) the situation. That means that the concept of adultery, standing alone, has no absolute meaning. It carries no moral value independently, only in the context of a situation.

Now, what happens when a situation actually arises? If some people say that adultery is wrong in situation "A" but right in situation "B", they are making an absolute statement about adultery in each particular situation. So they are contradicting themselves because they previously claimed adultery was relative.

You see, people can claim ethics are relative, but when they get to an actual situation, they still make absolute statements about ethics. The concept of relativism is self-destructive.

Perhaps a simpler way to look at it is this: Relativists say "there are no absolute truths." But think about this a moment. If I say, "There are no absolute truths," what kind of statement am I making? Obviously I am making an absolute statement about truth (i.e., that "there are no absolute truths"). But if truth is relative, then no absolute statements can be made. You see, if relativism is true, it is impossible to make any kind of absolute statement about truth—even the statement that relativism *is true*.

Absolutism: The Way God Intended It

Christianity opposes relativism at every turn because to surrender to relativism is to admit that truth does not have its source in God. It is determined by people and is wholly subjective in nature. According to relativism, there is no such thing as objective truth. Truth is wholly *subjective*—it is relative to individual or cultural interpretation.

The Bible, on the other hand, teaches that truth is *absolute*. It flows from a standard *outside* human reasoning and experience. Truth is complete, final, unchanging, and applies to everyone equally. Truth is not capricious nor is it relative and determined by individuals or cultures. Absolutism teaches that there exists an absolute standard for judging moral behavior and spiritual truth. This absolute standard is God, and He is revealed in Scripture (revelation). Hence God is the source of all truth, the ultimate reality, and the standard by which all truth-claims are measured. As Geisler observed, "Since God's moral character does not change, . . . whatever is traceable to God's unchanging moral character is a moral absolute."[8] In sum, if truth-claims do not measure up to God's revelation as recorded in the Bible, they are untruths and must be rejected.

Summary

Let's tie this all together. For something to be true, it must reflect the facts as they really exist. It is not enough to say that such-and-such is true because it agrees with the facts as *I understand them to be*. Rather it must agree with facts as they *really are*. It must correspond to reality. Truth does not change. As Geisler and Watkins put it:

> Truth, like ethical laws, is universal and corresponds to reality. Truth does not spring into existence, neither is it dependent on individuals, on cultures, or on what works. If a statement accurately describes or explains a state of affairs, then its meaning is true for all people, at all places, and in all time periods independently of anyone's knowledge or verification of the statement. Truth is timeless and absolute, and it corresponds to what is, not to what is not.[9]

Truth, then, is synonymous with reality. If you have truth, you have reality. This implies that if something was true in the past, it is true today whether I recognize it or not. Likewise, if something was false in the past, it is false today because truth is not affected by the passage of time or by personal opinion. It exists outside human beliefs, worldviews, cultures, or circumstances.

This is borne out in everyday experience. Occasionally, we discover that something we *thought* was true in the past turns out to be false. For example, a few decades ago it was believed that tomatoes were poisonous. Now we know tomatoes are *not* poisonous, and we recognize that this has always been true—even when we didn't know it. The truth that tomatoes are healthy food has nothing to do with time or one's beliefs.

What's Up Next?

Some readers will probably have noticed that although I have solved one problem (the fallacious nature of relativism), I have illuminated another problem. If truth is absolute and if the law of non-contradiction demands that only one religion can reveal the true nature of God and His relationship with humanity, why do people differ so drastically in their religious views?

The answer to this lies in understanding the difference between reality (what is really real—the actual state of the matter) and how people *interpret* reality, that is, what governs the way people *perceive* reality. This issue concerns worldviews, and it leads us to our next discussion.

CHAPTER FOUR

A World of My Own

Let's take a moment to review what we have learned so far. First, the modern world, not unlike the Roman Empire at the time of Christ, embodies a myriad of religious worldviews that all claim to represent truth. This pluralism is widely accepted among non-Christians. Consequently, because Christians claim that Christianity is the only true religion, many unbelievers not only reject Christianity, but they also view Christians as narrow-minded and exclusive.

Second, there are logical first principles which are the starting point of all truth and knowledge. Without them, it would be impossible to think and communicate rationally, to make sense out of the world, or to ever discover truth. It is because of these first principles, and in particular the laws of logic, that truth *can* be known.

Third, although we live in a world that increasingly holds to the philosophy of pluralism, nevertheless, truth is not relative but absolute. Truth corresponds to a reality that exists beyond and above human opinion and preference.

Fourth, since we know that truth is not relative and that there exist universal laws of logic that prohibit contradictory truth-claims from both being true, we can conclude that only one religion out of all contenders can reflect divine truth. God cannot exist in two or more contradictory natures. Just as you and I are unique individuals and can be identified only as ourselves, so too is God unique in His essential nature and can be identified only as He actually exists. God is either monotheistic or pantheistic or some other nature. There is only one God as Christians claim, or many gods as polytheists claim. God cannot be one and many at the same time. Thus, only one religion can reflect the true nature of God.

Someone may respond to this statement by asking, "Can't God be whatever He wants to be?" The answer is no. To say that God is sovereign and all-powerful does not mean that He can violate His essential nature. If God is good in His essential nature, He can't be the source of evil. If God is just in His essential nature, He can't judge unfairly. Likewise, the Bible teaches that God "does not lie or change His mind" (1 Sam. 15:29). Thus God cannot reveal Himself in contradictory ways in different religions. God is limited by His own nature.

With these facts established, the question becomes, Which religion is correct? Is God the God of the Muslims, the Hindus, the Polytheists, the Deists, the Jehovah's Witnesses, the Mormons, the New Age, the Christians—or is He the God of some other religion?

If God is ultimate reality and the source of absolute truth, then only God can answer this question. If we are to know truth about God at all, God Himself must reveal it to us.

Christians believe that the Bible is God's *only* written communication of revelational truth. Thus, the true nature of God is revealed only in the *Christian* religion. This being the case, all non-Christian religions are spurious, and absolute truth—religious, ethical, psychological, scientific—has its source only in the God of Scripture (Col. 2:3–4, 8).

But just claiming this does not automatically make it true. Most religions make similar truth-claims. My present task, then, is to establish a coherent system for determining truth that verifies Christianity and falsifies other religions. Christians cannot expect unbelievers to convert to Christianity unless they are convinced that Christianity reflects reality. As Francis Schaeffer put it: "Before a man is ready to become a Christian, he must have a proper understanding of truth, whether he has fully analyzed his concept of truth or not. . . . Our concept of truth will radically affect our understanding of what it means to become a Christian."[1]

This brings us to the topic at hand: worldviews. What people individually and culturally perceive as reality and believe to be true is largely determined by their particular worldview. Thus, if a worldview distorts reality, truth is likewise distorted.

This is nowhere more true than in the area of religion. If we are to successfully discover religious truth and if in particular I am to successfully prove the authenticity of Christianity, it is vital that we understand what a worldview is and the role it plays in influencing how people determine truth and interpret reality. Ronald Nash observed:

While all mature, thinking persons have a worldview, many of them are unaware of the fact. . . . One of the important tasks for philosophers, theologians, and, indeed, anyone interested in helping people in this important matter, is first to get people to realize that they do have a conceptual system. The second step is to help people get a clearer fix on the content of their worldview. What do they believe about the existence and nature of God, about humankind, morality, knowledge, and ultimate reality. The third step is to help people evaluate their worldview and either improve it (by removing inconsistencies and filling in gaps) or replace it with a better world view.[2]

What Is a Worldview?

Everyone has a worldview whether they realize it or not. What is a worldview? In the broadest sense, a worldview is the standard by which an individual, consciously and unconsciously, interprets *all* data so as to maintain a consistent and coherent understanding of the *whole* of reality.

A worldview acts like a filter in that it screens and analyzes and categorizes all information so that we can make sense out of the world. It is the frame of reference from which we discern truth from falsehood, make rational decisions, and formulate ethical and religious values.

Worldviews are made up of certain *presuppositions* or assumptions that an individual believes to be true. These presuppositions form the infrastructure of all worldviews. For example, Christians hold to the presuppositions that the supernatural world exists, that God is knowable, that Jesus is fully God and fully human, that heaven awaits us, and a host of other beliefs that are foundational and determinative to how Christians view religious, ethical, and other truths.

An opposite worldview is *naturalism*. Naturalism rejects the supernatural. Its presuppositions include the belief that the universe is eternal, that life evolved through random processes (evolution), and that the Bible is a book of religious experiences and creative writing—not divine revelation.

The key to understanding the role of presuppositions in worldviews is they are *taken for granted*. They are rarely defended, discussed, or analyzed because everyone who accepts them thinks they are necessarily true. And indeed, they *must* be true if a worldview is to accurately reveal truth as it really exists.

In one sense, it can be said that a worldview determines what *is* reality to an individual or culture. I need to be careful here. I am not saying that what we *think* is true via our worldview filter *actually is true*. I am saying that *supposed* truth is largely determined by our worldview presuppositions. This is why, given the same data, people with different worldviews reach different conclusions. Geisler and Watkins explained it this way:

> A world view is like a set of colored glasses. If one looks at the same object through green-colored glasses he will see it as green, while another looking at the same object through red glasses will see it as red. This is why people with different world views will often see the same facts in a very different way.[3]

A Moral Example

About thirty years ago a teenager in my extended family got pregnant out of wedlock. It was decided that she should have an abortion. At the time the family breathed a corporate sigh of relief. So did I. It seemed the easiest and most logical way to solve a messy situation.

Back then I didn't have a personal relationship with Jesus Christ, and I adhered to the world's values. I didn't see anything wrong with having an abortion. Today, however, I would do anything in my power to fight that decision (as would the person who had an abortion because she, too, is now a Christian).

What is different? The difference is that I have experienced a worldview shift. I now see the abortion issue through the filter of the Christian worldview rather than the secular worldview. So my opinion of abortion has made a complete reversal. The following chart helps explain this.

Views on Abortion

Christian worldview filter:	Atheistic worldview filter:
Assumes fetus fully human, has soul.	Assumes fetus pre-human, has no soul.
Conclusion: Abortion is murder.	**Conclusion:** Abortion like removing an appendix.

You can see that a worldview filter determines how an individual (as well as whole cultures) interprets data and makes truth decisions. But there's a problem here, and it's the key to understanding and confronting contradicting worldviews—and why it is *wrong* to claim that truth is exclusively the result of cultural worldview presuppositions.

The problem is this: What one *perceives to be true* through his worldview filter may *or* may not be true. In other words, to continue Geisler and Watkins's metaphor, a worldview acts like the lenses on glasses. The correct prescription makes things vivid and sharp. It reveals what's really there. But what if one's worldview filter is out of focus? An erroneous worldview filter will distort reality just as an incorrect prescription on glasses will prevent one from seeing clearly. In other words, if the worldview is in error, then what one thinks is true may be false.

Because people and cultures tend to judge reality only through the filter of their own particular worldview, they could be believing truth-claims (religious or otherwise) that are far removed from where truth really lies. Let me illustrate this with a fitting parallel that shows how a worldview can promote a *false* understanding of reality.

Counselors and therapists frequently deal with distorted worldviews, and they are very much aware of how these misperceptions can give their patients perverted views of reality. People whose childhoods were traumatized by physical or emotional abuse or who grew up in an environment lacking love and affection often become adults who carry around a suitcase full of misbeliefs about themselves and other people. These misbeliefs (analogous to distorted worldviews) prevent them from enjoying normal human relationships. It is the task of therapists to help their clients recognize this baggage, show how it prevents them from enjoying normal relationships, and then lead them through a healing process that results in a new worldview of themselves and others.

In a similar fashion, one of the tasks of Christian apologetics is to help unbelievers identify fallacious misbeliefs in the area of religious truth and then show how such erroneous beliefs garble reality. If it can be shown that the foundational presuppositions of a worldview are false, then the door is open for people to see that beliefs dependent upon that worldview are equally false. Doing this is a two-step process.

Truth Is Objective, Not Subjective

First, we must help unbelievers recognize when their existing worldview filter is interpreting truth subjectively rather than objectively. This happens when truth-claims are based on personal opinion and experience rather than on objective facts. Many people hold beliefs because of emotional commitment that has little or no bearing on reality.

Let me add quickly that subjective truth exists. But all subjective truth-claims must be qualified. We will look at this more closely in the following chapter when we examine religious experiences.

How do you determine if beliefs are grounded on emotional feelings or experiences rather than on objective facts? By examining the core presuppositions on which beliefs depend. A worldview often misconstrues reality (and hence truth) because it fosters truth-claims that rely on unsubstantiated presuppositions rather than on objective criteria that can be verified.

Here's the bottom line. Worldview presuppositions can be judged for truth only to the degree that they can be verified by objective evidence. If they can't, then there is no compelling reason to accept one worldview over another. To determine truth among competing religious worldviews, we must base our decision on which worldview best verifies its truth-claims.

The job of apologetics is to help non-Christians identify the erroneous presuppositions on which their religious or philosophical beliefs rest. If we can show that these assumptions are in error, hopefully the unbeliever will be willing to consider alternative views. This is a *key tactic* in offensive apologetics.

Take, for instance, the claim that Jesus rose from the dead. One can reject this truth-claim because it doesn't fit an anti-supernatural worldview that rejects the miraculous (naturalism). Or one can examine this claim according to the accepted canons of historical investigation and draw conclusions as to its truthfulness based on the evidence. Most readers will agree that only in the latter case can the truth of the Resurrection be ascertained.

Helping unbelievers determine the veracity and credibility of their own worldview is the assignment of the present chapter. To do this, we will examine negative and positive factors that influence worldviews. On the negative side, we will see the various ways in which a worldview can distort reality and lead away from truth. On the positive side, we will identify the ingredients that must be present before any worldview can accurately reveal truth.

Truth Can Be Tested

The second step in the two-step process of exposing erroneous worldview assumptions, especially in the area of religious truth, is to develop a standard for determining truth that is acceptable and applicable for all people *regardless* of their existing beliefs. This standard must appeal to our innate sense of reasoning so that we clearly see the difference between *truth* as it corresponds to reality and *error* as it flows from a worldview that *creates* its own false reality. This standard will provide a needed measuring stick for verifying or falsifying all religious truth-claims. This second step will be the job of the following two chapters. So let's return to our present task and examine the role worldviews play in determining truth.

Negative Factors Leading Away from Truth

It is possible for people to change worldviews. If it wasn't, evangelism would be a waste of time. Every religious convert experiences a change of worldview. Likewise, entire civilizations have changed worldviews. The Roman world in the early fourth century officially accepted Christianity as the state religion, ending centuries of pagan worship. As a result Christianity eventually became the dominant worldview throughout the Roman Empire and eventually all of Western civilization. Today, the Christian worldview has largely been replaced by secular humanism. Social, ethical, and religious practices are determined by people rather than God. Western civilization, then, has changed worldviews twice since the birth of Christ.

Similarly, the scientific community experiences worldview changes. Prior to Darwin, nature was seen as a textbook of God's general revelation, and divine creation was considered scientific fact. Today, science is firmly rooted in the philosophy of naturalism, and God has been removed as the creator and sustainer of the universe. Thus, since Darwin's time, science has made a complete worldview turnaround at a presuppositional level.

However, worldviews do not ordinarily change easily or gracefully. People are secure and comfortable in their worldviews (especially religious worldviews) and feel threatened when their beliefs are challenged. This should not be surprising, considering that one's worldview shapes and determines reality and what is perceived as truth (whether such truth is accurate or not). To question our worldview is to cast doubt on reality as we understand it.

But worldviews can distort reality and lead away from religious truth rather than reveal it. So if truth is to be discovered, it is important to recognize the negative elements that are characteristic in erroneous worldviews. There are four ways in which worldviews can lead *away* from religious truth.

The presupposition error. Although "a worldview provides an overall picture of reality into which one can fit all the pieces of life and the world,"[4] it is not necessarily an accurate picture of reality. A worldview rests on a foundation of specific presuppositions that may be absolutely true, partially true, or absolutely false.[5]

Because a worldview can pervert truth, some objective criteria is needed in order to test the veracity of its presuppositions. This is especially true when different worldviews have diametrically opposite views, as is the case of religious truth-claims.

Worldviews can be in error with regard to the subjective nature of their basic presuppositions. Therefore, they can lead away from truth. The historical truth of the Resurrection cannot be brushed aside simply because one's anti-supernatural presupposition *assumes* that miracles are impossible. Similarly, there must be an objective criteria for determining the veracity of all religious truth-claims. Worldview presuppositions need to be carefully examined in the light of objective, verifiable evidence that supports or condemns them.

The inconsistency error. The second factor that can lead *away* from truth is inconsistency. As pointed out, a worldview typically interprets data according to its own presuppositions. This is necessary in order to maintain internal harmony and consistency. For example, if a religious view claims that God is personal, to be consistent, God's role in creation, His relationship with human beings, the means to salvation . . . all such relevant doctrine must be in harmony with the nature of a personal God. If not, major inconsistences will flourish.

The danger here lies in the fact that a worldview can appear to be *internally consistent* but still be in error because it is *externally inconsistent*. Internal consistency alone is an inadequate test for truth. Here is an example of this.

New Age followers claim that humans are divine in their essential nature. This is internally consistent with the pantheistic concept of God endorsed by New Age religions. Pantheism teaches that all of reality is part of God's essence. Humans exist, so they, too, are part of God's essence. Thus humans are divine in their essential nature. But externally, this assumption falls apart. The claim that man is divine is not consistent with reality. No one can demonstrate objectively that he or she is divine. New Age followers can claim it, but they can't prove it. They can't even give concrete examples of it. So why should it be accepted as truth? We might just as well claim that we are Martians in disguise or that we can turn into a werewolf when the moon is full and no one is looking.

Christianity passes the internal consistency test. As Alister McGrath noted, "The Christian doctrines of God, the person and work of Christ, and of human nature, interact in such a manner as to give a consistent whole. If 'truth' is defined in terms of internal consistency, traditional Christian theology scores highly."[6]

Here is another inconsistency error. While attempting to maintain internal consistency, a worldview often creates truths from *within* its framework that may have no bearing on reality at all. This is an example of how a worldview actually *creates* a false reality.

Part of the problem here lies in the fact that all worldviews have a propensity to fit external data into their interpretive framework when that data may actually fit better in another worldview. Examples of this are legion, but let me share a common one from science.

Adhering to the philosophy of naturalism, science sees the origin of life as a process of time and chance independent of a creator God. Consequently, scientific discoveries in the area of origins are automatically made to fit within this evolutionary framework—*even if they fit within a creationist model better.* When this happens, and it does, the scientific worldview is not only inconsistent, but also it is guilty of foisting a false view of reality that is contradictory to truth.

Dr. John Warwick Montgomery gave a humorous anecdote illustrating people's penchant to make contrary objective data fit into their existing worldview presuppositions:

> Once upon a time there was a man who thought he was dead. His concerned wife and friends sent him to the friendly neighborhood psychiatrist. The psychiatrist determined to cure him by convincing him of one fact that contradicted his belief that he was dead. The psychiatrist decided to use the simple truth that dead men do not bleed. He put his patient to work reading medical texts, observing autopsies, etc. After weeks of effort, the patient finally said, "All right, all right! You've convinced me. Dead men do not bleed." Whereupon the psychiatrist stuck him in the arm with a needle, and the blood flowed. The man looked down with a contorted, ashen face and cried: "Good Lord! Dead men bleed after all!"
>
> This parable illustrates that if you hold unsound presuppositions with sufficient tenacity, facts will make no difference at all, and you will be able to create a world of your own, totally unrelated to reality and totally incapable of being touched by reality.[7]

The lifestyle error. The third way in which a worldview can lead away from truth concerns the lifestyle it promotes. An erroneous worldview can endorse moral and social standards that cause us to live lives that are not in our own best interest. Geisler and Watkins pointed out:

> One not only reads [interprets] through his worldview glasses, but also he *lives* by means of them. For a world view is really a world and *life* view. It includes within it value indicators or principles by which one makes value judgments.[8]

People's actions are largely controlled by their worldviews. What you and I consider morally and socially acceptable, what we crave materially, and the criteria for emotional and spiritual happiness are all dictated by our worldviews. Here are a few examples.

Westerners are programmed through their worldview to expect certain legal rights (such as religious freedom), to desire material possession (cars, a private home), and to have an unbridled opportunity to move upward on the social/economic ladder. However, cultures operating under different worldviews may see things differently. For example, under a communist worldview, religious freedom is a hindrance to the welfare of the state. For a Buddhist, material possessions interfere with spiritual growth. Historic Hinduism promotes strict rules (the caste system) that prevent one from advancing economically or socially.

But there is a problem with this pluralism of lifestyles. We have already seen that truth-claims that contradict each other cannot both be right. This means that a worldview promoting religious values and other beliefs that are inconsistent with what it really takes to promote human happiness and well-being is counterfeit and will ultimately fail to meet real human needs.

In the Christian worldview ultimate happiness and peace of mind are grounded in one's relationship with Jesus Christ. If this is true, nothing that happens in this world can remove this spiritual contentment (Rom. 8:37–39). On the other hand, if one's worldview erroneously teaches that happiness and peace of mind are in direct proportion to the quantity of one's material possessions or one's status in society, obviously such happiness will vanish if possessions or status are lost.

A worldview that endorses moral, social, economic, psychological, or other values and practices that are inconsistent with real human needs can only lead away from truth. To see this, look at practices in some non-Christian religions and ask yourself whether or not they further human welfare and peace of mind:

Are religions that reject medical aid for children contributing to human welfare? Are religions that ignore human suffering meeting human needs? Are religions that condemn and ostracize individuals for failure to perform rituals or for stumbling into sin really encouraging spiritual growth? Are human sacrifice, self-mutilation, neurotic submission to human authority, cutting family ties, confiscating one's personal wealth, degrading women, or promoting unattainable physical or economic goals ("health and wealth") really contributing to human happiness and well-being?

All of these are religious practices found in non-Christian worldviews. Clearly, none of them are in harmony with people's best interests.

The false-god error. The final way in which erroneous worldviews lead their adherents away from truth is the most important of all to identify. It centers on their view of God.[9] As mentioned previously, all major religions entertain widely different opinions concerning the nature of God and how He relates to people. Because a worldview's concept of God is foundational to all other beliefs, it dictates not only religious practices, but it also influences social, economic, and ethical practices. Here are a few examples.

In the Christian worldview, absolute standards of right and wrong originate in the divine mind and are not open to personal choice. A Christian's social, economic, and ethical behavior is strictly controlled by God's moral standards. Moreover, in God's eyes, men and women are equal (Gal. 3:28) and both possess intrinsic value. All people are worthy of care and compassion, and all are free to make personal decisions that affect their lives so long as the decisions do not hurt others and are not prohibited in Scripture (Rom. 14; 1 Cor. 8).[10]

In historic Hinduism the caste system limits one's economic and social freedom and individual worth. This social structure is a direct result of Hinduism's pantheistic concept of God and how this belief plays itself out in karma and the transmigration of souls. Likewise, in the Arab world, social, ethical, and even international relationships cannot be fully understood apart from the Islamic view of God.

What about a worldview that denies God's existence, such as secular humanism? Again, social, economic, and ethical behavior is directly related to its view of God (in this case, the belief that God *doesn't* exist). Here ethics are derived from the mind of people rather than from God. Without God there is no standard of right and wrong independent of human thoughts and experiences. Thus, as we've seen, ethics are relative, people have different views on what is right and wrong, and no one can logically claim that another person's moral principles are immoral. This means that the social, economic, and ethical practices advanced in Communism, Nazism, or democracy are equally credible.

Only God can be the absolute source of absolute truth. All truth must ultimately come from Him. If the true nature of God is distorted as it passes though the interpretative framework of a worldview, all other "truths" which are influenced or controlled by religious presuppositions are equally erroneous. It is inevitable that a worldview that distorts the nature of God will invariably pervert economic, social, moral, and all other practices.

It goes without saying that a worldview promoting an erroneous concept of God cannot lead to eternal salvation. A false God cannot redeem sinners or open the door to heaven.

Positive Factors Leading Toward Truth

There are three essential ingredients that must be present in any worldview before truth can be revealed. A worldview that lacks *any* of these characteristics must be seen as fraudulent and incapable of leading to truth, including religious truth. All worldviews must (1) be consistent, both internally *and* externally—their truth-claims can't contradict each other; (2) answer crucial questions about life and the cosmos that correspond to reality and human experience as universally understood and lived out; and (3) be emotionally and spiritually satisfying.

Is it consistent? For a worldview to accurately reveal reality and thereby point to absolute truth, it must be *internally* and *externally* consistent (coherent). By internally consistent, I mean that it must be obedient to the laws of logic that are innate to human consciousness and reasoning. For example, it cannot make contradictory statements such as, "people are 'little gods'" (i.e., both human and divine), or "ethics are relative" (an absolute statement about ethics). Unless a worldview adheres to the laws of logic, it will be irrational and unable to project truth.

By external consistency, I mean that a worldview must be true to the *facts* of history and science. As said, for example, a worldview can't simply reject the Resurrection in spite of historical testimony or reject Creation in spite of scientific evidence simply because they don't fit anti-supernatural assumptions. On the other hand, the facts of history and science must be understandable in context of the worldview. The Christian worldview must explain *why* the Resurrection fits the facts of history and *how* scientific evidence endorses Creation.

A worldview consistent with external reality will not fly in the face of what people universally experience and intuitively recognize as reality. I am not saying that truth is dependent on experience, but I am saying that a worldview will account for human experiences and not be contradicted by them. Let me return to a previous example to illustrate this.

Some pantheistic religions claim that pain and evil are illusions. However, all people respond to pain and evil as if they are real. For most people, this is adequate evidence to prove that pain and evil *are* real. They personally experience it. But for the sake of argument, let's pretend that pain and evil are illusions. Does this mean that pantheism adequately explains human suffering and evil? Absolutely not. Even if pain and evil are illusions, the *illusions* of pain and evil themselves are real. Thus, real or imagined, to be consistent with reality as universally understood and lived out, a pantheist must explain the presence of pain and evil. Pantheism is externally inconsistent with reality if it simply says that pain and evil are illusions and leaves it at that. People still hurt and suffer.

Does it answer crucial questions? All worldviews must *consistently* answer life's most perplexing questions and explain basic human traits. Many of these questions fall *beyond* the scope of science or philosophy: Where did I come from? Why am I here? Where will I go when I die? Why do people tend to sin? Why are people proud? Why do people seek power? Why do people covet what they cannot have? Or, on a more positive note, Why do people have the ability to reason? Why are people creative? Why do people crave love and sympathy?

More importantly, a worldview must explain about God: if He exists, the worldview must explain something of His nature; His relationship with people, both in this life and beyond; and His control (or lack of control) over history, creation, morality, and eternity. If God doesn't exist, a worldview must explain why people still believe in God and seek Him.

Answers to these questions have been eagerly sought throughout human history. Their universal appeal demonstrates the need for a universal answer. If a worldview flows from reality, it will satisfactorily and coherently answer all of these questions and more.

Is it emotionally and spiritually satisfying? The third necessary ingredient before a worldview can reflect reality and subsequently reveal truth is that it must be emotionally and spiritually satisfying. This means that it must answer the above questions in a way that is not only rational and in harmony with the facts of history and science (point one), but in a way that is subjectively true. For want of a better way to say it, a worldview will "feel" right. It will not leave one with nagging doubts as to truth.

How people feel about themselves, other people, and their status in society are directly related to their worldviews. Psychologically, then, a worldview is a filter through which people experience and express their innermost needs, such as love, acceptance, and a feeling of self-worth. Emotional needs are built into the human psyche, and an authentic worldview will provide for the fulfillment of these needs. A worldview that degrades humanity—such as Communism, Nazism, Hinduism, occultism, and countless other cults and religions—disqualifies itself as an authentic worldview because it fails to meet instinctive human needs.

Finally, and most importantly, a worldview will provide a medium to satisfy people's innate craving for spiritual fulfillment. God has placed within the consciousness of all people an intuitive awareness of His existence. An authentic worldview will provide a point of contact between God and His creation.

What's Ahead

As I have repeatedly emphasized, contradicting worldviews cannot all be true; only one can be true. If the Christian worldview is true, it alone reflects absolute reality—what is real about God, people, and life—and all other religions are false.

But how do we determine this? We have just examined the first step. A valid worldview must (1) avoid the pitfalls, the negative factors, that lead away from truth and (2) possess the positive factors that lead to truth: it must be internally and externally consistent; it must answer life's great and mysterious questions in a way that corresponds to reality; and it must be emotionally and spiritually satisfying. If you dig deeply enough, you will discover that only the Christian worldview fulfills all of these requirements. All other worldviews can be eliminated. This will become increasing apparent as you continue through this book.

If only one worldview can accurately reveal truth, there must be a way to determine this. Furthermore, this standard must be able to test *all* worldviews. Unless there is a measurement for truth that separates the one true worldview from all erroneous ones, the true worldview could not be identified and set apart. If Christianity is the one true worldview, it will not only possess all the requirements of an authentic worldview, but it will also verify its truth-claims in a way that other religions can't. It will pass the same truth tests that other religions fail.

This brings us to the second step in the two-step process of exposing erroneous worldviews. I have shown the requirements of a valid worldview, which Christianity possesses. Now I will present a standard for determining truth that will apply to all worldviews equally. To work, this standard must be (1) objective and verifiable, (2) precise enough so as to be unarguable in its conclusions, and (3) universal enough to appeal to the rational minds of all people, regardless of their presently held beliefs. This is the task of the next two chapters.

CHAPTER FIVE

Testing Truth-Claims for Truth

Most of us have heard the old fable about the five blind men who attempt to identify an elephant by touching different portions of its body. The first blind man feels the trunk and concludes the elephant is a snake. The second examines a leg and declares the elephant is a tree. The third touches the tail and claims the elephant is a rope. The fourth probes the elephant's side and believes it to be a house. Finally the fifth blind man handles the elephant's ear and asserts that the elephant is a fan.

Two aspects of this story parallel the problems we encounter when searching for religious truth. First, the five blind men's physical handicap can be likened to the blindness many people have due to erroneous worldviews. The five men *thought* they had discovered truth (identified accurately what they were feeling), but each man interpreted reality (the elephant) differently because their worldview filter (blindness) prevented reality from being known. If the elephant represents religious truth (i.e., Christianity), then what the five blind men *thought* the elephant was (tree, rope, etc.) represents false religious views. A worldview filters reality according to its own presuppositions, and if the presuppositions are false, truth—religious or otherwise—will be distorted. This problem was dealt with in the previous chapter, so let's look at the second aspect: the blind men's *methods* for determining truth.

The five blind men were limited in their search for truth to just feeling. Lacking a more accurate test for truth (such as sight) or some other means to verify their conclusions, it would have been virtually impossible for any of the blind men to have actually discovered that they were touching an elephant rather than a snake, tree, rope, house, or fan.

Like the elusive elephant, religious truth-claims are not readily subject to verification. In order to discover religious truth, it is vital that we identify and utilize the best truth-tests available. Because some methods for determining truth are not applicable to religious truth, we must also seek ways to *confirm* religious truth-claims through rational *and* objective methods.[1] Without such methods, there would be no way to ascertain which religion, among all contenders, possesses absolute truth.

What methods for acquiring truth (truth-tests), if any, are applicable to religious truth and which, if any, are subject to objective verification? Many truth-tests are relied upon by non-Christian religions as the basis for their truth-claims. If it can be shown that these tests are not applicable in the area of religious truth, it follows that the truth-claims resting upon them will likely be erroneous. Demonstrating the inadequacy of these tests, as they relate to religious truth, is a powerful argument against non-Christian worldviews. If a religion's *source* of truth is unreliable, its truth-claims crumble.

Ultimately, religious truth must be revelational. God can't be known by human reasoning alone. Indeed, God can't be known at all unless He chooses to reveal Himself. Religions may claim divine revelation, but they must be verified by using the following truth-tests. So in order to determine whether or not a particular religion's truth-claims *are* divine revelation requires that we analyze their means for acquiring truth.

Custom and Traditions

Customs are distinct behaviors that unite members within a group or culture and set them apart from other groups or cultures. When customs dictate behavior to the point that they become normative as unwritten "laws" passed down to succeeding generations, they become traditions. As an avenue of truth, it is assumed that because so many people adhere to a custom or a tradition for a long period of time, that custom or tradition represents right thinking and right behavior (truth). Millions of people can't all be wrong. I'm reminded of a bumper sticker I saw years ago: "Eat more lamb. A million coyotes can't be wrong!"

To some degree, customs and traditions play an important role in all religions. Most liturgical practices are part of religious traditions. Likewise worship services in most churches follow traditional patterns. In Roman Catholicism tradition has been formally recognized as an integral part of church authority.

The problem inherent in this view, however, is that customs and traditions, religious or otherwise, may not lead to right thinking or right behavior in spite of their acceptance. There have been many religious practices that were acceptable to "primitive" peoples that we find abominable today. No one in the civilized world, for example, believes that human sacrifices or self-mutilation or temple prostitution, as once practiced in some ancient pagan religions, are worthy of preservation or that such behavior reflects religious truth.

Generally speaking, however, there is nothing intrinsically wrong with religious customs or traditions if they serve the purpose of uniting or identifying practitioners—so long as they are in harmony with divine revelation. In other words, customs and traditions must flow *from* truth, not determine truth; customs and traditions are never a source of truth.

Authority

Closely related to customs and traditions is authority. Unlike customs and traditions, which we normally take for granted because that is the way things have always been, authority is a conscious surrendering of one's freedom to another individual or to a governmental or religious institution.

The problem with authority is that there is no guarantee that the person or structure in authority is presenting truth. A characteristic of all cults, for example, is the willingness of their followers to vest complete and autonomous authority on individuals whom they believe are the source of final and complete truth and whom they believe derive their wisdom from God.[2] This is done independently (and often in spite) of any criteria by which to demonstrate that this person warrants such devotion. The result is always the exaltation of the authoritarian figure and the degradation of the follower.

Cult leaders invariably seek whatever means necessary to preserve their authority, and independent thinking or disagreement is always suppressed. As a result, many bizarre beliefs and religious practices are common among today's cults—and many tragic happenings. Nearly a thousand followers of Jim Jones committed suicide because his authority became synonymous with religious truth. More recently, millions of TV viewers witnessed the tragic end of the Branch Davidians barricaded in Waco, Texas, because followers submitted to the sociopathic impulses of David Koresh.

To protect ourselves against authoritarianism, we must ask the same questions James Sire asked:

> Is there any reason to think that some religious figures have an insight into who God is and what he wants? Or any reason to trust what a Zen master says about the way

to peace? Here each teacher must be examined individually. Some may have far more likelihood of knowing what they are talking about then others. The fact that a teacher has followers points first to popularity, not to reliability. Is there any reason to think that any one or more of them really do have special knowledge? . . . Truth is the issue, not the source of truth.[3]

Humans (and human institutions) are fallible. Something beyond and outside human authority must be the criterion by which human authority is measured. Without such a standard, authority rests on the strongest, the smartest, the meanest, or the most politically powerful. Truth becomes relegated to personal opinion, not to an absolute that transcends human feelings and capriciousness.

Feelings, Intuition, and Common Sense

Although we can distinguish between feeling, intuition, and common sense, they are similar in their basic presuppositions. In all three cases, truth is apprehended subjectively by one's personal impressions or opinions. Of course, personal opinions are often in error. For example, common sense may dictate that the old adage "going around the mountain is faster than going over the mountain" is true, when in many cases it's false. You can hardly drive around the Rocky Mountains faster than you can drive over them. Maxims derived from individual experiences and touted as self-evident are not necessarily indicative of truth.

The problem with these methods of acquiring truth lies in their essential subjectivity. This results in many contradictory proclamations among religions.

One may feel that an inspiring thought is a direct revelation from God when the very thought may contradict the Bible or a host of other religious books. Some people believe intuitively that the better they are—the more good that they do—the better chance they have of getting into heaven. Yet the Bible teaches that it is not through *our* goodness that we are saved but through God's grace (Eph. 2:8–9). A Hare Krishna feels strongly that abstaining from meat and sexual activity (except for the purpose of having children) is necessary for a disciplined life. Some Christians will agree with this. Yet other Christians feel just as strongly that sexual activity and all foods are God's gracious gifts. Whose feelings are correct?

Nineteenth-century romantic John Muir once commented that "John the Baptist was not more eager to get all his fellow sinners into the Jordan than I to baptize all of mine in the beauty of God's mountains." Apparently,

Muir believed that people can feel closer to God in the mountains than in church. Other religions disagree. The Mormons hold their temples so sacred that non-Mormons are not even allowed inside.

In a similar way, feelings and intuition are an essential means of verifying truth in New Age religions. Many New Age followers claim that particular spots in Sedona, Arizona, possess powerful mystical energies that are conducive to meditation and to bringing one closer to the god-force (whatever that is). At such locales, they claim, one is much more likely to apprehend religious truth than elsewhere. But the reality may be that the only unique thing about these spots is that the devotee is standing over sandstone.

The problem is that feelings, intuition, and common sense are not self-authenticating; that is, because they neither encourage objective verification nor detect false impressions, they can just as easily lead to untruth as to truth. Once again, as with authority, there must be some verifiable criteria by which feelings, intuition, and common sense can be judged for their truth value.

Instinct

Instinct can be thought of as "programmed information." For instance, babies know instinctively to hold their breath when suddenly submerged in water. People know instinctively to drink when dehydrated rather than to eat. Kids (and tree-climbing animals) seem to naturally know from how far up a tree they can jump down without breaking a leg.

This kind of survival information is not truth in the sense that we are dealing with here. By programmed information I mean more than this: There are instinctive truths relevant to God and morality that are innate to all people.

The Bible teaches that there are spiritual and moral truths instinctive to the human race, and this is confirmed by secular studies. Like the Bible, anthropology and comparative religious studies teach that we instinctively recognize the existence of God and certain moral standards of behavior that are mandatory in human relationships. In at least these two ways, absolute truth is revealed in human instinct.

There are problems, however, with accurately *applying* these instinctive truths. Because of humanity's fallen state and because people are so easily persuaded by emotions and feelings, we have a proclivity to distort these two instincts and frequently end up worshiping false gods and endorsing immoral acts (Rom. 1:18–32).

Another problem is that instinct is incapable of revealing truth beyond its own limitations. Like information programmed into a computer, human instinct cannot offer truth beyond the purpose of its creation. Thus instinct may inform us that God exists and that He demands specific ethical behavior, but it does not give us information about the essential nature of God or clear information that leads to a saving relationship with God. This kind of information can only come from special revelation: objective, propositional statements from God that are recorded in Scripture and made alive in the person of Jesus Christ.

Pragmatism

The pragmatic approach to acquiring truth centers on a kind of utilitarianism. Something is true only so far as it is practical and serves a useful function. In particular, truth is determined by how well it meets human needs—not whether it flows from reality. Therefore, human experience becomes the testing ground for truth.

Actually, the pragmatic approach to truth is of some value in the religious arena. It highlights the value of religious experiences as confirming evidence for the existence of God. Nevertheless, pragmatism has serious drawbacks. Let's look at a few of them.

Norman Geisler offered a good summation of the merits and criticism of pragmatism.[4] Geisler pointed out that truth, as proclaimed by the pragmatist, may not be truth at all because it simply describes what works rather than what actually may be right. Amputating a finger to eliminate an infection, for example, may work in that it solves the infection problem, but a better (truer) way to solve the infection may be less costly (and painful). Likewise, stealing may provide one with an early retirement, but that does not make stealing right.

Geisler further explained that "truth may be unrelated to results. The results may have been accidental, in which case there would be no more relation to truth than accidentally discovering a million dollars proves one is the rightful owner of it."[5]

The most serious flaw of pragmatism in the religious arena lies in its inability to discern real truth from among contradicting truth-claims. A religion may appear to work because it meets the spiritual needs of its constituents, yet this does not automatically mean it reflects divine truth. Wrote Geisler, "Of course all truth must work, but not everything that works is necessarily true."[6] A counterfeit twenty dollar bill may buy a new hat, but possessing the hat doesn't make the twenty dollar bill real. It's still bogus, and eventually this will be discovered no matter how many people spend it.

Let me apply this to the problem at hand. Mormonism, Islam, and all other religions appear to satisfy practitioners' spiritual hunger. But if these religions are not from God, sooner or later it will become evident. The tragedy is that this discovery may not come until it's too late (Heb. 9:27). It is better to discover religious truth in this life and to be assured of eternal salvation in the next than to be content with just feeling spiritually satisfied now.

Actually a false religion is not spiritually satisfying; it is emotionally satisfying. It can't be spiritually satisfying if it's not from God—even if it feels right. Simply because Mormonism is family orientated and supportive of its members does not make the cult any more God's revelation of divine truth than a pain killer becomes a cure for cancer because it makes the pain go away.

The apostle Paul warned that even Satan can disguise himself as an angel of light (2 Cor. 11:14). The apostle John instructed us to "test the spirits to see whether they are from God; because many false prophets have gone out into the world" (1 John 4:1). This testing must rest on confirming objective evidence, not on apparent results.

Rationalism

This approach to acquiring truth has had a powerful influence in Western thought since René Descartes in the seventeenth century.[7] Its basic premise is that human reasoning, and human reasoning alone, is sufficient for acquiring truth.

It is important to understand the difference between reason and rationalism. Alister McGrath explained: "*Reason* is the basic human faculty of thinking, based on argument and evidence. It is theologically neutral and poses no threat to faith—unless it is regarded as the only source of knowledge about God. It then becomes *rationalism*, which is an exclusive reliance on human reason alone and a refusal to allow any weight to be given to divine revelation."[8]

Rationalists believe that ultimate truth is deduced from self-evident axioms that are innate to the human mind. Because these axioms are inescapably true, the conclusions deduced from them must also be true. Thus, truth is not derived from traditions, authority, intuition, instinct, experience, apparent results, or even empirical data, but rather from human logic reasoning from first principles.

There are two weaknesses with rationalism when applied to religious truth. First, rationalists put all their eggs in one basket. They stress that from self-evident axioms flow all truth. But what if these so-called self-evident axioms are false? The result, of course, is false conclusions.

There *are* logical first principles that are the cornerstone of human reasoning and that are necessary for coherent thinking. As we saw in chapter two, these first principles, which include the laws of logic, cannot be denied. They are part of *universal* human experience. But to go beyond them is to risk using a false system for determining truth that may not be true at all.

Rationalists offer no evidence to substantiate their first principles. If empirical or experiential evidence contradicts their axioms, this data is assumed to be incorrect because, to rationalists, human reasoning supersedes all other avenues of truth. Rationalists don't want to be bothered with the facts.

This obviously puts serious limits on discovering truth. If the so-called axioms cannot be verified, how do we determine whether they are true or not? We can't.

This brings up the second problem with rationalism. Professor Geisler pointed out: "Not only did the rationalists offer no demonstration of their axioms, but they differed in their conception of them and even drew differing conclusions from them."[9] Let me illustrate this.

It is in harmony with the concept of rationalism (although not all rationalists would agree with this) that God has placed in all human beings an innate knowledge of His existence and of certain of His attributes (Romans 1). This would be analogous to a universal axiom. But having this information a priori (existing in the mind at birth) does not mean that absolute truth about God will flow from it. Thus, as Geisler stated elsewhere, some rationalists "end up in pantheism, some in theism, [and] some with finite gods."[10]

As a test for determining truth, especially religious truth, rationalism fails. Its basic premises are assumptions, and these assumptions cannot be substantiated. Even when they are true, fallen humanity, more often than not, distorts them into erroneous conclusions. Thus rationalism is unable to demonstrate absolute religious truth. We can't reason ourselves to God. Somehow, religious assumptions must be tested by *objective* means if they are to accepted as divine truth.

Sense Perception

This method for procuring truth depends on assimilating data through our five senses (taste, touch, hearing, sight, and smell). Sense perception is vital to everyday living. For example, it is indispensable when it comes to protecting us from harm, such as tasting spoiled food before swallowing it or hearing a car's horn in time to jump out of the way. It also plays an important role in knowledge acquisition—your sense of sight is necessary in order for you to read this book and (hopefully) learn something new. The Bible also teaches that sense perception is important to learning (Matt. 12:3; 21:16; Mark 12:10; Rom. 10:14).

As a reliable interpreter of truth or as a means to *test* truth-claims, however, sense perception is limited and relativistic. It is limited because there is more to reality and human experience than what can be apprehended through our five senses. For example, sense perception is unable to verify ethical, psychological, or religious concepts. Likewise, sense perception is relativistic. People interpret the same phenomena differently. For example, our senses tell us that the air temperature is hot or cold. But hot to me may be comfortable to a Navaho, or cold to me may be invigorating to an Eskimo.

Likewise millions of people claim to have seen flying saucers—some even attach religious significance to them.[11] But upon investigation, it has been proven in many cases that the observer mistook an aircraft or some natural phenomena for the alleged UFO.

When my son was about eleven years old, he ran into the house one evening insisting that some kind of monster was lurking in a creek bed near our house. I got a flashlight, and we went out to investigate. The monster turned out to be the moon reflecting off a tree trunk.

And of course there are the hundreds of accounts of people "hearing" God or "seeing" Jesus—but never with a shred of evidence to prove that what they saw or heard was actually from God. In short, sense perception, standing alone, cannot be relied upon to give consistently reliable truth. Our senses can weave strange tales.

Experience

In his landmark book on religious experiences, philosopher and psychologist William James asked the question, "Is the sense of divine presence a sense of anything objectively true?"[12] In other words, are emotional or subjective encounters with God real? Can people experience God, or are all religious experiences psychological in nature and void of objective reality? And if real, do religious experiences "point to truth" or are they mere "pointers of truth"—do they reveal truth or confirm truth?

The answers to these questions make or break many religions. Why? Because personal religious experiences are the sacred cows of numerous religions, the entire basis of their truth-claims. Most cults have as their source of truth the religious experiences of alleged prophets. Similarly, personal religious experiences are the guiding force in many New Age religions and the so-called "World Faith Movement." Even well-established religions such as Islam and Mormonism rely on religious experiences as their cornerstone of truth. Concerning Islam, one author explained:

> The Koran . . . doesn't even attempt to give any reason for belief in its religion-ethical system (i.e., any solid evidence

strong enough to rationally support its command/reward structure). Rather, it claims, essentially, one will know it is true if one's heart is in the right place. Evidently there are people who can be successfully programmed, by just such a simple statement, to "experience" the required feelings.[13]

Now before going any further, I need to say this. Just because numerous false religions rely on religious experiences as their source of truth does not mean that all religious experiences are bogus. Nothing can be farther from the truth.

Many religious experiences *are* counterfeit (they must be if they endorse a false god or false religious system), but some are genuine personal encounters between people and God. It is undeniable that some religious experiences are real. They can't be brushed aside as mere psychological phenomenon, as some skeptics are prone to do. J. P. Moreland pointed out, "Such experiences are common to an overwhelming number of people and they're often life-transforming in a number of ways."[14]

What are these encounters like? As Moreland further explained, they may take various forms, but for most theists a religious experience includes "some sort of direct apprehension of a personal Being who is holy, good, awesome, separate from the subject, and One upon whom the subject depends in some way for life and care."[15]

Notice that this encounter does not include actually seeing God or hearing His voice. Nevertheless, a religious experience moves one beyond mere intellectual acknowledgment. It triggers an emotional or mystical response rather than a cognitive one. It confirms God's existence, His love and concern for His people, and His desire to have us walk with Him and to trust Him. Religious experiences, then, reveal truth *subjectively* rather than objectively. However, since I have previously expressed a concern for relying too heavily on subjectivism as a source of truth, we need to look at religious experiences critically—even Christian religious experiences.

Religious Experience and Christianity

No religion in the world would survive without confirming religious experiences. There must be more than intellectual dogma for a religion to be relevant and for it to inspire belief and acceptance. Even religions that do not emphasize a personal relationship with deity, such as many pantheistic religions, still maintain a subjective element to belief in which their god satisfies spiritual needs. This may occur in the here and now, as in Christianity, or only in some future state of bliss. But all religions answer life's great mysteries: Why am I here? Where did I come from? What happens to me after death? This is nowhere more important and evident than in Christianity.

Christianity rests on a solid foundation of history and can be verified by all the canons of historical investigation. But our faith also touches the heart as well as the mind. Religious experiences that reflect a true encounter with the living God are a vital ingredient of Christianity. More than any other religion in the world, Christianity confirms its truth-claims through profound, life-changing religious experiences. Jesus' disciples set the example for countless millions of Christians to follow.

Before Jesus was crucified, His followers abandoned Him, fled to their homes, and locked themselves inside from fear of the Jewish and Roman authorities (Matt. 26:56; John 20:19). Yet a few weeks later, these same men were bolding proclaiming the Christian message in the very city and before the very authorities who crucified Jesus. What caused this dramatic turnaround? What caused them to forfeit the comforts of life, their family and friends, and their traditional religious beliefs to embrace a religious movement that resulted in persecution and death? They encountered the living and risen Christ, and their lives were changed forever.

Over the past twenty centuries, millions upon millions of Christians claim to have experienced similar dramatic, life-changing, personal encounters with Jesus Christ. Not visible encounters, but spiritual encounters every bit as real and profound. Atheists and skeptics have become believers. Alcoholics and drug addicts have been set free from their dependencies. Marriages have been healed. Damaged relationships have been restored. Love, compassion, tolerance, and patience have blossomed where hate, greed, jealousy, and anger once flourished. It would be foolish to sweep aside such a magnitude of personal testimony as insignificant. Religious experience is powerful affirmation for the authenticity of the Christian worldview.

Unfortunately there are some misconceptions and misapplications of religious experiences among Christians. Generally, religious experiences *confirm* revelation (spiritual truths) not reveal it. David Wells noted:

> In any genuine knowledge of God, there is an experience of his grace and power, informed by the written Scriptures, mediated by the Holy Spirit, and based upon the work of Christ on the Cross. What is not so clear from the New Testament is that this experience should itself become the source of our knowledge of God or that it should be used to commend that knowledge to others.[16]

He later elaborated:

> Biblical faith is about truth. God has described himself and his works to us in the language of the Bible, and it is quite presumptuous for us to say that we have found a better way to hear him (through our own experience) and a better way to find reality (by constructing it within the self).[17]

The Dangers of Religious Experiences

Although religious experiences can be genuine encounters between people and God, it is dangerous to accept all religious experiences as valid. Both Shirley McLaine and Augustine had religious experiences, but obviously both can't reflect true encounters with God. This would require God to contradict Himself—a theological and logical impossibility. C. S. Lewis observed, "Religious experience can be made to yield almost any sort of God."[18] There are several reasons for critically examining all religious experiences, including Christian.

Counterfeit experiences. First, as indicated above, religious experiences are not restricted to Christians. Where there are counterfeit religions, there are counterfeit religious experiences. So having a religious experience does not automatically mean that it was a true encounter with God. Many religious experiences may be psychological in nature. Some people want to experience God so intensely that they actually imagine such an encounter. Worse yet, a supposed religious experience may be phoney. Many so-called prophets are no more than the worst kind of charlatan—outright frauds. Claiming to be speaking for God, they pretend to have had religious experiences in order to give authenticity to their teachings while, in fact, their goal is to bilk people out of their money and to promote their own selfish ambitions for power and control over people's lives.

Worse still, a religious experience may be the work of demons. Satan is described in the Bible as creating an image of himself as "an angle of light" (2 Cor. 11:14) while in reality he is the "father of lies" (John 8:44). It is not beyond his power to manufacture a phoney religious environment that promotes a false religious experience. In short, a supposed religious experience may be an encounter with the devil rather than with God!

Counter-conversions. A second danger inherent to religious experiences is what William James referred to as "'counter-conversions' . . . the transition from orthodoxy to infidelity." Wrote James:

> The new birth may be away from religion into incredulity;
> or it may be from moral scrupulosity into freedom and
> license; or it may be produced by the irruption into the
> individual's life of some new stimulus or passion, such as
> love, ambition, cupidity, revenge, or patriotic devotion.[19]

James is saying that a so-called religious experience may not be religion at all in the sense of an encounter with God or being morally righteous. The same psychological transformation ("new birth") one observes in genuine religious experiences may result in totally irreligious behavior.[20] What psychologically may qualify as a religious experience may lead away from truth rather than toward truth. It may lead to non-Christian religions or even to flagrantly immoral lifestyles. Again this illustrates the need for an objective criterion to judge the authenticity and truthfulness of all religious experience.

Contrary to logic. There is a third danger inherent to religious experiences that needs to be recognized. James pointed out that religious experiences can be so powerful and so compelling that they can cause us to disregard logic. The experience itself *becomes* reality:

> They [religious experiences] are as convincing to those
> who have them as any direct sensible experience can be,
> and they are, as a rule, much more convincing than results
> established by mere logic. . . . If you do have them, and
> have them at all strongly, the probability is that you can-
> not help regarding them as genuine perceptions of truth,
> as revelations of a kind of reality which no adverse argu-
> ment, however unanswerable by you in words, can expel
> from your belief.[21]

The danger here is obvious. If a religious experience does not have its source in God (truth), then its source is from something other than God. We saw previously that there are only two other possibilities: the experience is either wholly psychological in nature and has no bearing on reality at all, or it is demonic in origin. In either case, a religious experience can feel so real that we do not want to be "bothered with the facts," that is we refuse to judge the truth of the experience against common sense logic or contrary objective evidences (such as Scripture). This clearly leaves us wide open to any manner of bizarre and perverted beliefs.

Although religious experiences can be, and often are, direct means for apprehending *insights* into truth, they should never be considered the *source* of truth. Experiences *affirm* truth; they give powerful supporting evidence for truth. Yet in and of themselves they do not give truth. Religious experiences should correspond to reality but not create reality (which, incidentally, is exactly what some religions claim they do).

Christians claim that Jesus changes lives. If this is true, we should see innumerable examples of changed lives in those who have met the living Christ—which is exactly what we do see. But the historicity of Jesus and His claim to deity do not rest on personal experience alone but on concrete historical facts. This is quite different from what is found in other religions.

If the Bible is God's Word, it will be the qualifier of religious experiences—the standard or framework by which all religious experiences can be measured for truth. If a so-called religious experience is not in harmony with Scriptures, it must be rejected. God's subjective revelation through the Holy Spirit will never contradict His objective written and recorded revelation in Scripture.

Religious Experience and Other Religions

This brings up an important question. Can religious experiences outside of Christianity reveal the true God? J. P. Moreland gave an excellent response, so I'll let him answer for me:

> It may well be that God is experienced in some cases of numinous [spiritual] experience in different world religions. . . . This does not mean that such airiness is vertical and it certainly does not mean that they would bring salvation. Christianity teaches that salvation comes only through faith in Christ. But just as a red table is being experienced by a person even though he is color blind and describes the table as a brown ellipse, so God may be the real object of some numinous experiences (one could not rule out other spiritual beings such as demons as appropriate objects in these cases) even though the descriptions are not completely accurate. At some point, a line would be crossed where we would no longer say that God is being perceived. If one ascribes barking and a tail to the table we would say that the subject is hallucinating. Similarly, if one ascribes contradictory or monistic properties to God, we would not say that God is not being attended to accu-

rately in these cases but rather that he is not being attended to at all.[22]

God will *never* allow Himself to be identified with a false religion or reveal Himself in a fashion that is contrary to His essential nature as revealed in Scripture. Nor will He reveal spiritual truths contrary to His revelation in Scripture.

Religious Experiences and Evangelism

As we have seen, religious experiences are *personal*, and it does not logically follow that they are always expressions of divine truth. Thus it is impossible to argue, on a purely subjective level, that one's personal religious experiences are valid or invalid. We are dealing with feelings, not facts. Experience only proves that you had an experience.

This has a direct bearing on evangelism. If Christians cannot rely on religious experience as their sole source of absolute truth or to verify their truth-claims, neither can they rely on religious experience as their only tool for evangelism. It is difficult for many unbelievers to accept religious experiences as evidence of religious truth. This is why personal testimony based on past religious experiences—although an important ingredient in evangelism—often fails to convict unbelievers.

Christians are on the same wave length with other Christians. When we claim to experience, for example, the "peace of Jesus" or the "filling of the Holy Spirit," other Christians know precisely what we mean. They acknowledge the truthfulness of this experience because it fits in their worldview and they too have experienced it. But atheists can't identify with this experience. They will interpret this "religious experience" as a response to *natural* phenomenon. To them, a religious experience is no more than a psychological episode created out of an emotional need. Likewise, deliverance from alcoholism or a healed marriage can be accounted for naturally, that is, in a non-spiritual way. Atheists will always vie for a nonsupernatural explanation.

Religious experiences are always subject to a variety of possible interpretations, and these interpretations are largely determined by our worldview. We can't expect unbelievers to feel the same convincing emotions we feel when they do not have the indwelling Spirit of God (1 Cor. 2:14).

Changed lives provide compelling and powerful evidence for the truthfulness of Christianity. However, personal testimony is not the only tool for evangelism, and sometimes it is not even the best. Of course it will be effective for individuals whom God chooses to convict in that fashion. But many unbelievers need supporting evidence to confirm religious experiences. They can't emotionally relate with the experiences of others, no matter how amazing and spiritual such experiences are. Call them tough-minded or left-brained, they simply need more evidence than the accounts of personal religious experiences to convince them of the truthfulness of Christianity. Effective evangelism requires going the extra mile with such tough-minded individuals by providing them with the objective evidence they demand (i.e., apologetics).

This brings us back to the need for an objective method to substantiate religious experiences. It is up to the Holy Spirit to touch unbelievers' hearts with truth. It is up to us to carefully examine these experiences to see if they are of God. It is not axiomatic that all religious experiences have their source in God. Psychological need, demonic deception, or something else may be the source of some so-called religious experiences. Hence it is vital that we seek and employ some means of discerning whether our religious experiences flow from God or from some other source.

The Scientific Method

Truth, if it is to be acknowledged and accepted by all people as universal truth, must stand up to critical scrutiny; it must be able to be tested. We have seen that truth doesn't flow exclusively from customs and traditions; authority figures and institutions; feelings, intuitions, and common sense; instinct; pragmatism; rationalism; sense perception; or religious experience. These truth-tests serve only to confirm truth, not reveal it. We are left with only one remaining truth-test. It is the only valid and reliable way to determine truth: the scientific method.

Let me say at the outset that I am not endorsing the philosophy of science or the naturalistic conclusions of science. The scientific worldview is subject to many distortions that evolve out of its erroneous presuppositions. But I am suggesting that the *scientific method* for discovering truth is the most reliable method because *it alone can be tested*. The scientific method, although encompassing some difficulties, is overall the most reliable method for acquiring truth. John Warwick Montgomery affirmed this position:

> Empirical or scientific method is the truly valid way of approaching truth because it alone can accomplish to the satisfaction of all what the other methods . . . cannot; not only do its results not need to be tested for error independently, but is in itself capable of determining what author-

ity to follow and what common sense beliefs and presuppositions to hold.[23]

I am going to postpone a full discussion of this truth-test until the following chapter because it needs to be examined in more detail than the other tests. For now, I will highlight its main tenants.

The scientific approach to acquiring and testing truth comprises two important principles that we will discuss in the following chapter: evidence and probability. As a system, the scientific method involves inductive reasoning, that is, accumulating reliable evidence that points to a general conclusion based on the highest degree of probability attainable.

Although probability leaves the door open for error, it is the closest we can come to absolute truth outside of self-evident or self-defining first principles. Probability conclusions, derived from objective evidence, are the most trustworthy method there is for acquiring and testing truth. They reveal the clearest and most logical choices between conflicting alternatives.

Almost all decisions in life are based on probability, whether they involve scientific matters (all scientific laws are based on probable results); legal matters (we send people to prison based on the preponderance of evidence—probability); historical matters (we evaluate historical evidence and draw conclusions based on the probable accuracy of documentation); or personal matters (we determine our chances of crossing the street safely).

We live in a world in which scientific proof is the accepted model for truth verification. As one observer put it, we look upon science with a sort of uncritical reverence. Because scientific thought has become the paradigm through which truth is sought, it behooves us to use this model whenever possible to increase our chances of gaining a hearing with unbelievers. If non-Christians believe that the scientific method is the only path to truth, let's walk that path with them and show that it too leads to Christ.

Most of the unbelievers who ordinary Christians encounter in the workplace, among family and friends, or while participating in evangelistic outreaches are non-religious, secularized people programmed to believe whatever dogma science touts. These individuals may not accept our presuppositions (rationalism), our arguments that Christianity works (pragmatism), or our religious experiences ("I've heard them all before and they mean nothing to me"), but they may listen if we point out that Christianity is supported by facts and that these facts can be verified using the scientific method of investigation.

Hence, the scientific approach is the most effective way to gain the ear of an unbeliever. It is trustworthy both in defending the Christian worldview and in testing worldviews promulgated by non-Christian religions.

Is More Better?

Before examining the scientific truth-test in detail, I want to address a question that may have occurred to some of you: If we combine all the above methods for discovering and testing truth-claims, will we not discover the most comprehensive method of all?

This idea sounds reasonable and is endorsed by some apologists. However, it does not logically follow that if one method for acquiring truth is inadequate standing on its own it becomes useful if used in conjunction with other systems. If I have shown sufficiently that the various methods for acquiring and testing truth are individually inadequate, then it follows that any combination of them will be equally inadequate. A multitude of little wrongs only adds up to one big wrong, not a right.

A worldview that depends largely on any of the above truth-tests (other than the scientific), such as authority or experience, should not be trusted. All non-Christian religions rely on one or more of these inadequate methods for acquiring and testing truth. Hence, all non-Christian religions must be in error so far as the source of absolute religious truth. Let me put this as a syllogism:

Premise one: All worldviews that rely on inadequate truth-tests are in error.

Premise two: All non-Christian religions rely on inadequate truth-tests.

Conclusion: All non-Christian religions are in error.

There is some merit in appropriating the better features of some of the above truth tests, but only so far as they contribute to a coherent worldview and can be tested using the scientific method—and so long as they are used to confirm truth, not act as a source of truth. Religious experiences give an existential verification that the Christian worldview is true. They show that Christianity meets human needs at the deepest level. Likewise the use of deductive logic, as endorsed by the rationalists, is helpful in showing the coherence and logical nature of the Christian worldview. And as any Christian will verify, Christianity works; it's pragmatic.

But false religions also boast of religious experiences, profess to be logically coherent, and claim to work—and their beliefs contradict Christianity. Since only one religion can represent truth, more than experience, rationalism, and pragmatism is needed to demonstrate absolute truth. There must also be objective, verifiable evidence.

If truth were subjective and without verification, there would be no way to determine religious truth at all. We might as well throw up our arms in despair and reject all religions. The alternative is to arbitrarily sample several options and choose the one we like best. But this smacks of pragmatism, and truth would be abandoned in favor of personal preference. The process of discovering truth cannot move forward unless it steps on the firm ground of objective, verifiable evidence.

If you and I are to bet our eternity on a particular religion, we had better have reasons for why we believe as we do. The only way to confirm religious truth is to examine the qualifications of the various contenders to determine which religion can validate its claims. I believe that the way to do this is through the scientific method. It is trustworthy both in defending the Christian worldview as well as in testing worldviews promulgated by non-Christian religions and secular philosophies.

CHAPTER SIX

The Whole Truth
and Nothing
but the Truth

Like many new believers before me, I became interested in apologetics in part because of my inability to respond to challenges critical of Christianity. I remember two comments particularly well. One came from a relative who had studied world religions for many years. He made this comment with all the authority of a Bible scholar: "Jesus never *really* claimed to be God. Nowhere in the Bible does He say, 'I'm God.'" Although I was certain that Jesus *did* claim to be God (if not in those exact words), I was nevertheless taken aback. And I was unable to prove him wrong.

The second comment that helped spur me into a study of apologetics expresses a common attitude among many unbelievers, especially those who look to science as the ultimate purveyor of truth. I was on vacation with an old friend, and we were eating dinner at a restaurant overlooking the Pacific Ocean in Fort Bragg, California. I was a new Christian, and after hearing me share my faith my friend responded, "I wish I could believe . . . if I only had proof."

Well, I had no proof either. I only had faith. To him, this amounted to no more than personal opinion. He needed more than a testimony to convince him of the authenticity of Christianity.

Because of these and other questions—which I *knew* Christianity had answers to, but to which I personally couldn't respond (and I admit because of *my own* need to confirm that Christianity was rational and not a leap of blind faith)—I began to study apologetics. People wanted proof, and I was determined to give it to them. I looked to apologetics as proof of Christianity.

One of the first lessons I learned after beginning my studies was that proof, in the sense that my friend wanted it, was considered by many Christians as impossible to give. Apologetics, I was taught, doesn't *prove* anything, in the sense of absolute proof; it doesn't give irrefutable proof with no possibility of error. It can't prove with absolute certainty, for example, that Jesus Christ is God or that Christianity is the only true religion.

Religious truth-claims are not true by definition, as in mathematics (five times five can only be twenty-five) or tautologies (all husbands are married). Nor can religious truths be proven scientifically through observation and experimentation. Religious truths fall outside the category of absolute certainty. Thus apologetics, most apologists agree, consists of giving *evidence* supporting Christian truth-claims, not proof positive. This is why many apologists use the phrase "evidences for Christianity" to describe apologetic conclusions rather than claiming "proof of Christianity."

But after many years of apologetic studies, I disagree with this position. Apologetics *can* prove the authenticity of Christianity! I am not saying that Christian truth-claims are self-evident like mathematics or tautologies. But I am saying that apologetics can prove Christian truth-claims *if* we use the word *proof* in the same sense that we use it in all other areas of knowledge that do not entail mathematics or formal logic. It is perfectly legitimate for Christians to claim that they can *prove* Jesus is God and that Christianity is the only true religion. This is no semantics game I'm playing. I'm not equivocating—I'm not redefining the meaning of *proof*. I intend to use it exactly as it is used in other areas of truth and knowledge.

What Is Proof?

There are different levels of proof, or certainty, that are relevant to specific areas of knowledge and not to others. When we attain the highest level of certainty possible in any one particular area of knowledge, we have realistically reached truth because we cannot demonstrate a higher level of certainty. For all practical purposes, in that we accept this same level of truth in everyday matters and make decisions accordingly, we have reached absolute certainty.

If this sounds confusing, look at it like this. We can't expect one level of certainty (i.e., mathematical certainty) to apply to all areas of knowledge. There are areas of knowledge in which mathematical and logical inferences play no part and are not even applicable.[1] What we accept as historically true, legally true, and scientifically true do not and cannot depend on absolute proof in the form of logical and mathematical certainty.

Yet we accept historical, legal, and scientific truths without question. Why? Because the preponderance of evidence and our personal experiences have confirmed their dependability (truthfulness) beyond reasonable doubt. Almost all matters of fact rely on probability confirmation.[2] We accept data that flows out of these three categories of truth in spite of the lack of absolute certainty. Let me cite a few examples.

No one rejects the truth that George Washington, Abraham Lincoln, and most other historical figures lived, although no one alive today has ever seen them. No one argues that a man can't be found guilty of a crime that wasn't witnessed if sufficient evidence demonstrates his guilt. No one denies the scientific fact that the sun is ninety-three millions miles away from earth although no one has paced it off with a yard stick. None of these facts are certain in the absolute sense of the word. People accept them as true because the weight of the evidence is so overwhelmingly convincing— highly probable. Granted these facts may *not* be true, but to deny them— or similar truth-claims—because they are not mathematically certain would be tantamount to denying virtually everything we believe. We couldn't function in the real world with such skepticism. We couldn't even eat a hamburger because we couldn't be absolutely certain it wasn't poisonous.

Let me put this another way. Let's say someone claims that he once owned a red Ford truck, and we challenge him to prove it. The ex-Ford truck owner provides evidence of such overwhelming reliability that there appears to be absolutely no chance that he is lying. He produces a color photograph with himself standing next to a red Ford truck dangling the keys. He provides a sales contract with the vehicle identification number, a physical description, and his signature as purchaser. He shows us insurance papers and eyewitness affidavits vouching to his ownership. Most people would consider such evidence proof equivalent to "absolute certainty" because they could not imagine that so much evidence could be in error. But does all this evidence constitute absolute proof? Not at all!

I don't want to get silly in my illustration, but consider this. There is always the *chance* that the ex-Ford owner has fostered a clever scam. Maybe the photograph is of someone else's red Ford truck with his picture taken by it. Perhaps his legal documents were forged, and he bribed the eyewitnesses. Maybe all the eyewitnesses were hallucinating and just thought they were seeing a red Ford truck when it was really a green Chevy van. Maybe the ex-Ford truck owner is an invader from a parallel universe and doesn't exist in our reality at all!

The point is this. Regardless of how remote, there is always the *possibility* that what we believe is factual is actually in error. But if we lived with such skepticism and accept truth-claims only to the degree that they are mathematically or logically certain, we would never believe anything in history, accept any scientific theories, or convict anyone of a crime. As Ronald Nash put it, "Once one leaves the arena of purely formal reasoning for the world of blood, sweat, and tears, one is required to abandon logical certainty for probability."[3]

Let me tie this to religious truth-claims. Christianity can provide the same degree of proof—that is, the highest level of certainty possible—for the deity of Jesus Christ, the reliability and authenticity of the Bible, and other Christian truth-claims that are used to prove beyond doubt most other facts that we take for granted in our everyday lives. Furthermore, no other religion in the world offers this same level of certainty.

The Whole Proof and Nothing but the Proof

This brings us to two very important points. First, people can make such a powerful *emotional* commitment to a belief that no amount of rational argumentation or contrary evidence will change their minds. They literally "don't want to be bothered with the facts." In such cases, lack of conviction is not due to lack of evidence but to dogged devotion to a personal belief. As Geisler wrote:

> Lack of persuasion is not necessarily a fault of rational proofs as such; it is a result of persons' own choice. In order for proof to be persuasive there must be a cooperation of the will with the mind. If one is unwilling to look at a proof, unwilling to accept any proof, unwilling to accept the validity of a proof as applied to God, or unwilling to accept the God the proof concludes, then one will not be persuaded by theistic arguments. On the other hand, persons of good will who are seeking the truth will be persuaded by good reasoning.[4]

The second point is that when people demand proof of Christian truth-claims, without realizing it they switch from accepting the kinds of proof they accept in other matters to demanding absolute certainty. Thus, when a non-Christian wants proof that the Bible is authentic or proof that Jesus is God, what he really wants is mathematical certainty. But as we saw, this is impossible to obtain because mathematical certainty is an entirely different category of proof than what is used to establish historic, legal, scientific, *and* religious truths. Mathematical proof does not pertain to these areas of knowledge. This does not mean proof is impossible, only that it is not proof in a mathematical sense.

In light of all this, the first task in witnessing to unbelievers may be to help them to see that absolute certainty is *not* available as proof for *any* religious truth-claims—including Christian—but it is likewise not available as proof for most other truths we take for granted. Nevertheless, religious truth-claims *can be* proven, and to a level of certainty that is just as valuable and applicable in the area of religion as absolute certainty is in mathematics and pure logic. This same degree of certainty—and not more— is used to prove practically all historical, scientific, and legal truths that we believe and take for granted. It is in this sense that we can honestly and legitimately assert that we can *prove* Christian truth-claims.

The kind of proof I'm talking about depends on accumulated evidences, and its conclusions are based on probability—the highest level of certainty possible in the area of history, law, science, and religion. From the start, however, it needs to be understood that probability is only as good as the soundness of the evidence on which is depends. This leads us to our next topic: What constitutes sound evidence and probability conclusions?

Evidence

Nineteenth-century Harvard law professor Simon Greenleaf, considered one of the greatest American authorities on the use of evidence in legal procedures, stated that *"a proposition of fact is proved, when its truth is established by competent and satisfactory evidence"*[5] [emphasis his]. He then went on to define what constitutes competent and satisfactory evidence:

> By competent evidence, is meant such as the nature of the thing to be proved requires; and by satisfactory evidence, is meant that amount of proof, which ordinarily satisfies an unprejudiced mind, beyond any reasonable doubt. The circumstances which will amount to this degree of proof can never be previously defined; the only legal test to which they can be subjected is, their sufficiency to satisfy the mind and conscience of a man of common prudence and discretion, and so to convince him, that he would venture to act upon the conviction in matter of the highest concern and importance to his own interest. If, therefore, the subject is a problem in mathematics, its truth is to be shown by the certainty of demonstrative evidence. But if it is a question of fact in human affairs, nothing more than moral evidence [probability] can be required, for this is the best evidence which, from the nature of the case, is attainable. . . .

When we have this degree of evidence, it is unreasonable
to require more.[6]

In other words, the nature of proof required in religious matters is not
mathematical certainty but confirming evidence. And the amount of evidence required is that which leads to a conclusion beyond reasonable doubt.
Now what would constitute this kind of evidence? More than anything
else, sound evidence would include eyewitness testimony, reliable documentation, and scientific and historical confirmation. It would also be
philosophically and logically consistent with human experience (blaming
a murder on an alien, for example, would not be in harmony with human
experience). This is precisely the kind of evidence on which we make our
daily decisions and on which truth is determined in most areas of human
activity. As Greenleaf put it, evidence convinces us to take action "in matters of the highest concern and importance to [our] own interest."[7]

Probability

Simon Greenleaf had this to say about probability:

In all human transactions, the highest degree of assurance
to which we can arrive, short of the evidence of our own
senses, is that of probability. The most that can be asserted
is, that the narrative [i.e., the Bible] is more likely to be
truth than false; and it may be in the highest degree more
likely, but still be short of absolute mathematical certainly.
Yet this very probability may be so great as to satisfy the
mind of the most cautious, and enforce the assent of the
most reluctant and unbelieving. If it is such as usually satisfies reasonable men, in matters of ordinary transaction,
it is all which the greatest skeptic has a right to require;
for it is by such evidence alone that our rights are determined, in the civil tribunals; and on no other evidence do
they proceed, even in capital cases.[8]

Greenleaf reminded us that people do not have infinite and absolute
knowledge and therefore must accept or reject truth based on the evidence
available. Furthermore, the probability of truth is based on the volume of
evidence amassed for or against it. This is nowhere more evident than in
religious truth. As Carnell put it, "Proof for the Christian faith, as proof for any
worldview that is worth talking about, cannot rise above rational probability. . . .

The more the evidence increases, the more the strength of probability increases."[9]

To put it another way, the power of probability lies in its cumulative testimony. Here is a helpful illustration used by Ronald Nash, quoting from Richard Swinburne's *Existence of God*:

> That Smith has blood on his hands hardly makes it probable that Smith murdered Mrs. Jones, nor (by itself) does the fact that Smith stood to gain from Mrs. Jones' death, nor (by itself) does the fact that Smith was near the scene of the murder at the time of its being committed, but all these phenomena taken together (perhaps with other phenomena as well) may well indeed make the conclusion probable.[10]

The fact is, probability controls human actions in almost every area of life. Response to probability is so intrinsic to our human psyche that we take if for granted and seldom think about it. We automatically and subconsciously make decisions according to their probable outcome. The examples of this are endless. When we get into an automobile, we do not calculate our chance of having an accident—although we know that possibility is real. We do not turn on a light switch wondering if the power is on—although it may not be. We eat in restaurants trusting in the probability that what we eat is not poisonous. We drink water from the tap trusting that it is probably safe to drink. We marry on the probability that we will be compatible for life. Doctors prescribe medicine based on the probable outcome of their diagnoses. In no case can any of these decisions be based on absolute certainty. A hundred times a day we make decisions based on their probable outcome, all the while acting as if these decisions were at the level of absolute certainty.

In sum, most of the actions we take and the decisions we make in our lives are grounded in our belief that the probable results are reliable and predictable. In our normal activities and decision making, we accept the probable just as readily and completely as we accept mathematical certainties. We rely on probability as absolute proof in the sense that we trust it and think of it as the highest level of certainty available to whatever truth question is at hand. This concept is so important to apologetic evangelism that I want to drive it home with two more illustrations.

ing Decisions

which we can make decisions: (1) absolute
probability. Let's look at absolute certainty

othing except the conclusions of mathemat-
he outcome is axiomatic or self-evident in
esults in absolute certainty. In every other
ion short of absolute certainty. So if we set
based solely on absolute certainty, we would
er than, for example, balancing our check-
ands are married, triangles are three-sided,

ss I'm absolutely certain it will not break
f the lot, I would never buy a car. Unless
a crime, no one would ever be convicted.
if I refused to believe in God unless I saw
iod. Absolute certainty must be ruled out as
ions—including religious ones.
Do we normally make decisions—especially
as religious matters—based on their *possi-
bility*. If I pick up a ....., there is a possibility it won't bite me. But
just knowing this is possible does not encourage me to play with rattle-
snakes. It's possible that bloodletting may cure a potentially terminal disease, but wise people seek medical attention. It's possible the Greek god
Zeus exists even though there is no evidence for it. I think you get the
message. We don't make life's decisions based on their possible outcome.

We seek truth based on the third alternative: probability. We make the
majority of life's decisions based on their probable outcome.

Let's say you are driving on the freeway through downtown Los Ange-
les at five o'clock Friday afternoon. Everyone is rushing to get home, and
the freeway is packed. Suddenly you run out of gas and are forced to pull
over to the center divide. Across the freeway is an off-ramp leading to a
service station. You think to yourself, If I get down in a sprinter's stance,
close my eyes, and go for it, I may make it across the four lanes of freeway
and survive to get gas!

There is that *possibility*, but would you attempt it? Not if you're in your
right mind.

Let's change the scene. This time you are in a country village with only
one main road. It's three in the morning and not a single car is in sight. You
run out of gas and see a twenty-four-hour service station across the street.

But you are an unusually cautious person (more accurately, an unusual person) and will not make any decision unless you have absolute certainty of the outcome. In this case, you want to be absolutely certain that you will not be killed crossing the empty street. Would you cross? The answer has to be no! Why? Because there is always the *possibility* that at the very moment you step into the street, a meteorite plunging to earth will crash in the exact spot you are crossing.

This may sound far-fetched, but I'm sure you see my point. Regardless of how unlikely it is that a meteorite will strike you, nevertheless, there is the remote possibility that it may. (Believe it or not, there is at least one documented case of this actually happening.[11])

In both of these scenarios, there is an overwhelming *probability* of the outcome of your choices. In the first case, you will probably be flattened if you blindly dash across an L.A. freeway at five o'clock on a Friday afternoon. On the other hand, it is extremely unlikely that a meteorite will strike you anywhere on earth at any time.

By necessity, we make everyday decisions based on probability, not on absolute certainty nor on possibility. In the real world, probability guides us to truth in most areas of knowledge.

If we apply this principle to religious truth and use the same criteria for determining religious truth that we use to determine truth in non-religious areas, we can *prove* the authenticity of Christianity. To demonstrate this, we will examine three areas in which we depend entirely on probability in order to determine truth and then apply them to the question of religious truth.

Scientific Proof

If we ask the question, By what criteria do rational people determine what is factual and what is false? the most common response is whether or not it can be proven scientifically. We are a generation taught to respect the "assured results" of science, and in Western culture people tend to think that truth should be established according to the canons of scientific verification. Science is looked upon as *the* absolute authority.

Does science offer proof in the sense of absolute certainty? Exactly what can science prove? The fact is, science does not offer absolute certainty at all. It only gives evidence that points to absolute certainty.

Science is normally trustworthy with regard to data that can be tested through observation and experimentation—things that can be repeated. As we saw in the previous chapter, the scientific method is the most reliable means for determining truth in matters that are not logically or mathematically self-evident. But the scientific method does not reach conclusions on a level of certainty equal to mathematical proof.

The scientific method entails the idea of accumulating and testing data in order to reach the highest degree of probability. This method can be applied to practically every area of knowledge, not just to science (history, law, psychology, religion, etc.). But again, the scientific method does not lead to absolute certainty even in the area of science. Why? Because the conclusions of science are probable and can change as new scientific evidence surfaces. Let me give an example of this.

For three hundred years, from the time of Isaac Newton (1642–1727) to the twentieth century, science taught that nature adhered to unchanging natural laws. Nature was seen as orderly, predictable, and as functioning much like a machine. Due to new findings in quantum physics, however, nature is no longer viewed as orderly and predictable, at least in the subatomic realm. Science recognizes that today's laws and theories may not be applicable in the future. Natural laws are seen as *descriptions* of how phenomena function rather than predictions of *how* they will function. An experiment may yield the same results a thousand times in a row, but on the next test, an anomaly may appear. Montgomery observed:

> In the case of every theory involving statements of fact, proof is impossible, for new information may always turn up to disprove previous findings. Since this is so, all science and history—indeed all intelligent decisions between alternative theories, beliefs, ideologies, must rest squarely upon probability.[12]

Notice that Montgomery used the word *probability* to describe the category of proof that validates science (and history). We do not casually reject scientific claims because they lack absolute certainty, rather we accept them because of the *probability* of their certainty.

This brings us to the question of whether or not the scientific method for acquiring and confirming truth can be applied to religious truth. The answer is yes. Although we cannot prove religious claims scientifically in the same way that we can prove that water boils at 212 degrees Fahrenheit at sea level (observation and experimentation), we can apply the scientific method to religious truth-claims. In other words, we can accumulate and analyze evidence in order to reach the highest level of certainty possible.

When we apply this method to religious truth, we have valid criteria for determining the truth of the existence of God, the deity of Christ, and the reliability of Scripture. We also have valid criteria for comparing the contradictory claims of various religions. That belief system that provides verifiable, objective evidence has the highest probability of being spiritual truth.

Admittedly this does not result in absolute truth in a mathematical sense, but there is no better *objective* way to determine religious truth.

Do you see how this works? A single evidence supporting the deity of Jesus Christ or the historical reliability of the Bible may not be convincing. But on the strength of accumulated evidence, we reach a compelling level of probability that equals the same degree of proof that we have in scientific matters. We can be just as sure that Jesus is God in light of the overwhelming evidence confirming this as we can that eating fatty foods and smoking cause heart disease. Both are probable conclusions, and both can be tested for accuracy by examining the evidence. The difference is that one is tested through observation and experimentation, and the other is tested by historical, legal, and other criteria. In both cases, however, the highest level of certainty available is used to prove truth-claims. Because no higher level of proof can be applied, the conclusion must be accepted as absolute—if truth is to be settled at all. The alternative is to never have religious *or* scientific truth.

Have I Left God Behind?

This approach to religious truth will offend some people. At first blush, it may appear that I have removed completely the work of the Holy Spirit as the agent of conviction. I do not mean to imply this. I fully understand and agree with the fundamental Christian truth that no one becomes a Christian independent of the work of the Spirit of God (Luke 24:45; Acts 16:14). Moreover I am not saying that faith is unnecessary in receiving Jesus Christ as Lord and Savior. Faith is always present when we make decisions based on probability because the possibility factor is always present. In a contingent universe, anything is possible. Because probability is not mathematical certainty, faith is the bridge one must cross to go from probability to belief. The Bible clearly teaches that a step of faith is empowered only by God (1 Cor. 12:3). But the Bible also teaches that faith comes through knowledge (Rom. 10:14–17).

The goal of apologetics is to identify and remove obstacles to faith. To achieve this, we must frequently meet non-Christians on their own turf. This means, among other things, communicating at a level and in a manner they will listen to and understand. The scientific method to discovering religious truth is designed to do exactly that.

The Spirit of God can and does work in many ways—even in ways that do not always include a specific gospel message or traditional Bible language or personal testimony. We put God in a box and limit the work of the Holy Spirit when we insist that God is unable to work in the lives of unbelievers except through personal testimony and *The Four Spiritual Laws*. God works through a variety of messages and circumstances.

The job of apologetic evangelists, then, is to be an instrument of the Holy Spirit. This means that we strive to create an environment in which God is set free to work. Like the apostle Paul, we must become "all things to all men, that [we] may by all means save some" (1 Cor. 9:22).

Legal Proofs

Another example of the kind of proof I am talking about is found in our legal system. Law professor John Warwick Montgomery observed: "Legal reasoning operates on *Probabilities*, not possibilities: preponderance of evidence in most civil actions; evidence beyond reasonable (not beyond *all*) doubt in criminal matters."[13]

Here's how probability determines truth in legal reasoning. Beginning with the unbiased assumption that defendants are innocent until proven guilty, our courts set out to determine the fate of the accused based on the evidence marshaled against them. For example, a civil case is won or lost based entirely on the "preponderance" of evidence. If 51 percent of the evidence is against the defendant, that person loses.

An even higher standard of proof (but still based on probability) is required in criminal cases. Suppose a murder has been committed and a suspect apprehended. The case goes to trial. Now to have *absolute certainty* that the suspect is guilty, the jury would have had to witness the crime. Obviously this is impossible; otherwise, the jury would be witnesses rather than a jury (and this still would not amount to absolute certainty—it is always *possible* the witnesses might be mistaken).

What criterion does our court system use to determine the guilt or innocence of a defendant? The term is "proof to a moral certainty beyond reasonable doubt." This means that there must be no other reasonable explanation for the crime other than that the accused did it. The prosecutor builds a case by presenting such an impressive and compelling amount of evidence that all other possibilities are eliminated. In short, the accused is sent to prison or even executed, not according to absolute certainty, but according to the preponderance of evidence. Moral certainty is not absolute certainty—there is always the remote possibility that the defendant may be innocent. But it is the highest level of certainty attainable in the area of legal truth. If the courts tried for a higher level of proof (i.e., mathematical proof), truth would be unattainable.

Legal reasoning as a means to determine religious truth is of tremendous value in two ways. First, Christianity is the only religion in the world in which truth-claims can be tested by legal reasoning, that is, by evidence. All other religions require us to accept their tenets based either on the testimony of their founders and leaders (authoritarianism or rationalism) or on our own personal experience. However, in all such cases, "testimony" is incapable of validating truth. Religious authoritarians rarely, if ever, try to verify or defend their authority. Rationalists promote contradictory conclusions that flow from fallible human beings. And religious experiences may *endorse* religious truths, but in and of themselves, they are unable to give religious truth.

The second value of legal reasoning in the area of religious truth is that it provides a way to show unbelievers that absolute proof, in the mathematical sense, is not the criterion for ascertaining religious truth. Most unbelievers think they should be given 100 percent proof (absolute mathematical certainty) for the authenticity of Christianity. Yet this kind of proof is not available or even expected in our legal system. Legal decisions, like our day-to-day decisions, are *always* based on probability.

Let's apply this to Christianity. A person demands absolute proof that Jesus rose from the dead. We point out that the Resurrection was a historical event and can't be repeated. Thus it can't be proven in a mathematical sense (by experimentation and observation). However, we continue, we can prove the Resurrection in a legal sense. We do this by presenting all the evidence that supports the Resurrection and refuting all the so-called evidence that argues against it. In other words, we show that the biblical explanation of the Resurrection is the paradigm that *best explains* all the facts (the empty tomb, the changed lives of the apostles, the beginning of the Christian church, and so on). If the preponderance of evidence supports the biblical claim that Jesus Christ rose from the dead, we are justified to accept this as absolute truth in the same way that we accept that people are guilty of crimes based on the preponderance of evidence marshaled against them. In both cases, we have the highest level of certainty available in the area of legal truth. For all practicable purposes, we have "absolute" proof. If we reject the evidence for the Resurrection, to be consistent, no criminal should ever be convicted of a crime.

Eyewitness Testimony

In a court case, what kind of evidence is most condemning so far as establishing the probability of guilt? Although circumstantial evidence can play a significant role, by far the most important evidence a prosecutor can muster is eyewitness testimony. Now note this. The most compelling and irrefutable evidence for the resurrection of Jesus Christ comes from recorded eyewitnesses (legal testimony). The major events in Jesus' life—

His miracles, teachings, trial, death, and post-resurrection appearances—are recorded either by eyewitnesses to the events or by the companions of eyewitnesses. In a court case, the New Testament Gospels are primary source material, not second- or third-hand information and not oral tradition.

The authors of the New Testament were careful to note this eyewitness testimony in order to validate the authenticity of their writings. The apostle Peter wrote, "For we did not follow cleverly devised tales when we made known to you the power and coming of our Lord Jesus Christ, but we were *eyewitnesses* of His majesty" (2 Peter 1:16). The apostle John is even more specific: "What was from the beginning, what we have *heard*, what we have *seen* with our eyes, what we beheld and our hands *handled*, concerning the Word of Life . . . what we have seen and heard we proclaim to you also" (1 John 1:1–3, emphasis mine).

Simon Greenleaf, in his work *The Testimony of the Evangelists: The Gospels Examined by the Rules of Evidence,* wrote of the apostles' integrity. Greenleaf concluded:

> They had every possible motive to review carefully the grounds of their faith, and the evidence of the great facts and truths which they asserted; and these motives were pressed upon their attention with the most melancholy and terrific frequency. It was therefore impossible that they could have persisted in affirming the truths they have narrated, had not Jesus actually risen from the dead and had they not know of this fact as certainly as they knew any other fact. . . . And their writings show them to have been men of vigorous understandings. If then their testimony was not true, there was no possible motive for its fabrication.[14]

If the case for Christianity were to go through the rigors of our court system and all the evidence available were presented, there is little doubt that the resurrection of Jesus Christ (the absolute proof of His deity—Romans 1:4) would be considered proven "to a moral certainty beyond reasonable doubt." The historicity of Jesus' resurrection is proven to the highest level of certainty possible.

On the basis of legal evidence alone, it is clear that Jesus Christ is who He claims to be: God incarnate, the risen Messiah, our Lord and Savior.

Historical Proofs

The third area in which probability plays a crucial role in determining and sustaining truth concerns historical facts. How do we know Abraham

Lincoln, Napoleon Bonaparte, Julius Caesar, Siddhartha Gautama (the Buddha), Jesus Christ, or any other historical figure ever lived? How do we know the *Mayflower* landed at Plymouth Rock in 1620? How do we know Joan of Arc was burned at the stake in 1431? None of these events can be confirmed by science because they are not repeatable and observable events. Yet we believe all to be historical facts. Why? Because they are substantiated by probability evidence.

Once again, as in science and law, historical conclusions are not dependent on absolute certainty as in mathematics or formal logic. However, as Habermas and Miethe have stated:

> The concept of probability does not preclude our achieving certainty in matters of well-established historical findings [e.g., the testimony of Scriptures]. Events that are validated by careful historical research (and especially those established for long periods of time) in the absence of contrary findings are proven facts.[15]

As in science and law, historical investigation is carried forth by employing the same sort of verification techniques used in almost all the affairs of life. Christianity demands nothing more than what is applied to other areas of human knowledge; it needs no greater test to authenticate it than what is used to authenticate scientific, legal, and now historical matters.

How do responsible historians work? They adhere to two important rules. First, they are unbiased in their approach. They do not allow their own presuppositions to influence their investigation or their conclusions. They hold to the conviction that the truthfulness of any historical event depends on the preponderance of evidence supporting it. So they investigate and analyze all pertinent evidence.

Second, in order to determine fact from fiction, historians seek the best evidence available to support or disavow a particular event. What kind of evidence is best? There is only *one* kind that is reliable enough to determine beyond reasonable doubt the factuality of any historical event: primary source evidence (firsthand testimony). This entails recorded documentation by qualified and honest eyewitnesses to the event. If observers are psychologically sound and do not disqualify themselves by contradictions, inaccuracies, opposing evidence, or obvious bias, their testimony is considered valid to substantiate truth. The most convincing and irrefutable historical incidents rely on this kind of documentation.

Can this be applied to Christianity? Absolutely. I will illustrate this with an example.

All Christian truth-claims ultimately rest with the reliability of the Bible. What we know about the nature of God, deity of Christ, work of the Holy Spirit, means to salvation, answered prayer, and all other Christian truths rests squarely on the authenticity of Scripture.[16] If we cannot sustain the Bible's authority and reliability, Christianity crumbles. Its truth-claims would then rest on the subjective religious experiences or the personal interpretation of people—which, we saw, *cannot* be tested independently for truth. It is the reliability of the Bible that sets Christianity apart from all other religions.

The Bible is a historical document that Christians claim is the revelation of God. Its authors are dead and much of its contents are not only fantastic, but impossible to prove with mathematical certainty (e.g., miracles, deity of Christ, and creation). How does historical evidence prove the reliability and authenticity of the Bible? It does so in two ways.

First, it reveals positive evidence. The same methods of historical investigation used to determine the authenticity of any ancient document can be applied to the Bible. The results of this investigation demonstrate beyond doubt that the Bible is completely accurate and trustworthy with regard to its textual composition, its historical, scientific, and prophetic claims, and its geographical and cultural descriptions. Here are a few examples.

Archaeology has verified almost all the historical events, peoples, nations, cities, and customs portrayed in Scripture. Many of these facts were once rejected by skeptics because, for centuries, their existence was mentioned only in the Bible. Likewise, hundreds of Old Testament prophecies have been borne out by history.[17] Most noteworthy are the dozens of prophecies that predict the coming, life, ministry, death, and resurrection of Jesus Christ.[18] All together, these and other historical evidences are powerful and compelling proof of the historicity of the Bible.

What conclusion can we draw? In every area in which it can be checked out, the Bible is proven to be totally reliable. If its verifiable contents are proven to be accurate and reliable, it is logical to assume that its subjective truth-claims (i.e., its spiritual contents) are equally trustworthy. There is no logical reason to reject this. The key here is that the Bible's subjective truths do not attempt to stand alone. They rest squarely and firmly on a foundation of verifiable facts.

Second, historical investigation provides negative evidence. When the same techniques of historical investigation used to verify the Bible are applied to other religious documents, the non-Christian documents are found to be spurious. Much of their historical, scientific, and prophetic claims are false. Indeed, all non-Christian religions are conspicuous by the *absence* of historical evidence. Ultimately, non-Christian religions fall back on personal experiences and the unverified so-called "revelations" of their religious leaders.

No other religious book in the world passes the test of objective historical investigation that the Bible does. As such, Christianity attains the highest level of certainty available in the area of historical proof.

Closing Thought

The job of apologetic evangelism is to encourage unbelievers to consider the evidence for Christianity and to make faith decisions for Christ based on the assurance (the highest probability) that Christianity is true. On the flip side, we also encourage unbelievers to see that other religions are false because they lack the scientific, legal, and historical evidence that supports Christianity.

Evidence alone will not lead one to make a faith commitment to Christ. No one makes such a decision unaided by the Spirit of God. Nor can a person who doesn't have the indwelling Holy Spirit experience the subjective confirmation that a Christian can (Rom. 8:16; 1 Cor. 2:14; 1 John 4:13).

Nevertheless, on a purely intellectual level, unbelievers can recognize the truth of Christianity and can conclude that if divine revelation exists at all, Christianity is it. They can do this because all human beings have a God-given capacity to reason by virtue of being created in His image. God designed us to love and accept Him with our minds as well as our hearts (Mark 12:30). By applying this reasoning capacity to religious matters, people searching for truth can check the facts and verify or falsify Christian truth-claims before ever committing themselves to becoming Christians. This doesn't mean that they *will then choose* to become Christians, but it does show that their decision will not be a leap of blind faith. The decision rests on facts.

The job of apologetics is completed when intellectual obstacles (real or imagined) to faith are removed, thereby creating an environment in which the Holy Spirit is free to work. But it is always the job of the Holy Spirit to convict and convince the unbeliever of saving truth.

PART TWO

"You shall know the truth, and the truth shall make you free."
—*John 8:32*

We have reached a point in our study where it's time to apply what we have learned. Truth, as we've seen, is absolute—it's perfect and complete. It's not relative in the sense that it flows from human or cultural bias or depends on individual situations. Moreover, truth can be known. It corresponds to reality. It is unchanging and universal in application. And it never violates the laws of logic. Except in the areas of mathematics and formal logic, truth is the highest level of certainty attainable in any area of knowledge under investigation. This is probability. Finally, truth can be tested. It is verifiable through objective evidences via the scientific method.

This concept of truth fits perfectly with the Christian worldview. So the issue we turn to now is whether or not *other* worldviews are equally coherent and consistent with objective reality. If they are not, we have demonstrated that the Christian worldview *is* reality and non-Christian worldviews are erroneous.

In the next chapter, we will examine the main tenets of the Christian worldview. Then in the following five chapters we will examine the most prevalent and influential worldviews competing with Christianity in modern society: pantheism (especially the New Age Movement); Christian cults;

naturalism (the philosophical basis of modern science); secular humanism (the prevailing "religious" faith in Western society); and postmodernism (an evolving form of secular humanism supported by the presuppositions of pluralism and relativism).

My intention in part 2 of this book is to demonstrate that if we follow the criteria for determining religious truth as outlined in part 1, we will see that none of these worldviews reveal religious truth. In order to establish this, we will examine six key issues that must be addressed in any worldview that wishes to be considered a candidate for truth: (1) the nature of God (if they believe in His existence—if they don't, why not); (2) the nature of humanity; (3) the origin of life and the cosmos; (4) the source of evil and suffering; (5) the eternal destiny of humanity (extinction or afterlife); and (6) a verifiable source of truth.

These six issues are addressed in most worldviews, and together they answer life's most important and perplexing questions: Who am I? What is my status in relation to the rest of life and the cosmos? Where did I come from (what is the origin of my existence)? Why am I here (what purpose do I have for my existence)? What happens to me when I die (is there life after death, and if so, how do I obtain it)?

Does Beating Opponents Make Christianity True?

Before getting started, I need to make an important clarification. I am not trying to verify the authenticity of Christianity by merely demonstrating the fallacious nature of opposing worldviews. There is an inherent weakness in this approach.

In a contingent universe, a continuous flow of competing and contradictory religious worldviews can exist. Christians may adequately demonstrate the erroneous nature of every *known* non-Christian worldview, but there is always the possibility that yet *another* will surface out of the matrix of human imagination and claim to be ultimate reality. It's impossible, therefore, to demonstrate the authenticity of Christianity just by attempting to refute every spurious religion and philosophy that comes down the pike.

The Christian worldview, like any other worldview, stands or falls according to its own internal and external consistency—not on the fallacious nature of other worldviews. Consequently, the ideal way to defeat conflicting worldviews is not to strike them down one by one but to show the veracity of Christianity with regard to how it corresponds to reality and passes the truth-tests outlined in the previous chapters.

In the following chapters, I will compare Christianity with its chief competitors, not just to show the bogus nature of the non-Christian views, but to verify the Christian position by demonstrating that it alone is internally and externally consistent and corresponds to reality as universally understood and lived out.

Don't Make Me Mad!

From the perspective of evangelism, this approach has an important psychological advantage. None of us likes to hear negative things about our beliefs. Hammering on unbelievers about the inconsistencies of their worldview may close the door to dialogue rather than open it. When we are put on the defensive, we are often more concerned with not looking foolish than with listening to truth. On the other hand, establishing the veracity of Christianity by showing its consistency with reality and by sharing its rational explanations to life's crucial questions not only confirms Christianity, but it does so in an inoffensive way. Still, it is virtually impossible to share the positive elements of Christianity without contrasting them with the negative elements of non-Christian worldviews. Error is more clearly seen when contrasted with truth. Thus it's essential, to be effective in apologetic evangelism, that individual Christians become familiar with the non-Christian worldviews they daily confront and learn how they differ from Christianity. The following chapters will enable you to understand and to respond to how most unbelievers view reality—what is real to them—especially in the area of religious truth.

CHAPTER SEVEN

Christianity: God Is God

Religion is more than information about the nature of God or how to receive eternal life. A religion is a world-and-life view. It must integrate and explain the entire fabric of reality. This is why, if a religion truly reflects divine revelation, its essential doctrines (its objective truth-claims) will generate subjective responses in the forms of emotional, psychological, and spiritual fulfillment. If they don't, we have compelling reasons to reject that religion for promoting beliefs and practices not in harmony with reality or human nature.

For example, if a religious worldview is true, its concept of worship *must* lead one closer experientially to the living God. Its moral mandates *must* lead to a more fruitful, joyful life. Its perceptions of evil *must* reflect actions that lead away from God and toward both earthly and eternal suffering.

Both the objective and subjective truth-claims in the Christian religion are in perfect harmony with human needs and with reality as most people understand it. We want to determine whether *other* worldviews (both religious and secular) reveal objective and subjective truths with equal or greater veracity. To answer this, we will examine six essential ingredients found in all worldviews, starting with Christianity.

The Nature of God

Christians are monotheists who recognize (through divine revelation) the Trinitarian nature of God. There is one God in essence, power, and authority who eternally exists as three distinct, coequal personalities: Father, Son, and Holy Spirit. This does not mean that Christians believe in three gods (polytheism). Rather, the doctrine of the Trinity reveals that there is only one God who exists in three distinct persons, and that all three share the same divine nature. All three persons are the one God.

How do we know this? Because the Bible clearly states that God is "one" (monotheism—Deut. 6:4), yet the attributes of God the Father, God the Son, and God the Holy Spirit are identical. All three are self-existent, eternal, omnipresent (present everywhere at once), omniscient (have all knowledge), omnipotent (all-powerful), and sovereign—attributes exhibited only by God. The only explanation for this is that the one God eternally exists as Father, Son, and Holy Spirit. Let me put this as a syllogism to make it clear:

Premise one: Only God is omniscient, omnipresent, omnipotent.
Premise two: The Father, Son, and Holy Spirit are all omnipresent, omniscient, omnipotent.
Conclusion: God is triune.

The triune nature of God is just one revealing characteristic of the Christian God. He is also distinct from other so-called "gods" by virtue of being both *transcendent* (He is creator of the universe and thus distinct from His creation—Gen. 1:1; Isa. 55:8–9; Rom. 11:33–34) and *immanent* (He actively upholds and maintains the universe—Col. 1:17; Ps. 139:7–8; Luke 12:6–7). His transcendence and immanency are reflections of His self-existence, eternality, omnipotence, omnipresence, omniscience, and sovereignty.

God is also holy (Lev. 19:2; 1 Peter 1:15). Thus He is morally perfect in truth and goodness and separated from all evil. God is righteous (Ps. 11:7; 119:137; 145:17). Thus He is just and fair and not capricious. God is the essence of love and long-suffering (1 John 4:16; 2 Peter 3:9). Thus all people have the opportunity for forgiveness. Yet God can tolerate no sin (Rom. 1:32; 6:23). Thus unrepentant sinners will ultimately be punished. God is personal, and we can have a personal relationship with Him (Matt. 6:9; Rom. 8:15; 1 Cor. 6:19). Thus He acts on His own incentive, sovereignly and purposefully working in the lives of people, calling them and revealing Himself to them. Yet He also responds to their individual needs (John 14:13–14; James 5:16). Thus He answers prayer and performs miracles.

Nowhere is our personal relationship with God more wonderfully revealed than in the person and work of Jesus Christ. In the Son, God entered history by taking on the body of a man (Phil. 2:6–7). Thus Jesus Christ is God in human flesh (John 1:1, 14; Col. 2:9; Heb. 1:3), fully God and fully human. In Christ, God is revealed explicitly, directly, and visibly. If we want to know God, if we want to understand what God is like, if we want to grasp how God wishes us to live, if we want to fathom God's plan for salvation, if we want to enjoy a personal, active relationship with God, we need look no further than Jesus Christ.

Jesus separates Christianity from all other religions in the world. No religion but Christianity reveals the *real* Jesus, and no religion but Christianity worships Him as the eternal God.

The Nature of Humanity

Humans are created in God's image (Gen. 1:26). This means several things. For one, we are unique and of more value to God than other created things (Ps. 8:5; Luke 12:24). Moreover, we are distinct from the rest of creation in that we possess the "communicable" attributes of God. Unlike animals, for example, we have a moral conscience (Rom. 2:13–15), a free will (Gen. 2:16–17; Rom. 1:18; Eph. 4:18), the capacity to think and reason (self-awareness—2 Peter 2:12; Jude 10), and the ability to love (1 John 4:7–8, 19) and strive for holiness (1 Peter 1:15).

Unlike God, we possess a natural tendency to sin. We can hate, lie, and perform other acts out of character with the nature of God. Moreover, unlike God, we are *not* sovereign over our own lives. We aren't immortal or divine: God is creator, we are created. We don't possess a single attribute that distinguishes God as God (e.g., omniscience, omnipotence, omnipresence, sinlessness, holiness, eternality). Indeed, with regard to purely *physical* creation, we are no different from the rest of animal life (Eccl. 3:19–20). That we live at all is only by the power of God (Acts 17:25). That we have "dominion" (i.e., stewardship responsibilities) over nature is because we were given such authority and responsibility by God (Gen. 2:15; Ps. 8:6).

Origin of the Cosmos

The world is not eternal. It had a specific beginning and it will have a specific end. God is the creator and sustainer of nature and of all life (Col. 1:16–17). This means that God not only created the universe *ex nihilo* (out of nothing that preexisted—Heb. 11:3), but He also created the natural laws that hold the universe together and allow the earth to function in ecological harmony. In short, God is the source of all that is (Acts 17:25).

Suffering and Evil

The question of why there is evil and suffering in the world is of such importance that I want to allocate more space to explaining the Christian view of it than I have to other doctrines.

When God created the earth and life, He said that it was "very good" (Gen. 1:31). The earth was a place free from sin, evil, and human (and animal) suffering. Yet today, we all suffer emotional and physical pain, are subject to diseases and natural disasters, and are victims of evil and perpetrators of sin. What caused God's perfect creation to turn sour?

The historic entrance of evil and suffering into the world is explained in the biblical account of the Fall. Rather than quote Bible verses, let me tell this gripping story in narrative form (primary texts are Gen. 2:4–3:24; Isa. 14:12–15; Rom. 5:12–19).

God created Adam and Eve—the first human couple. God did not create them because He was lonely, for He is perfect in the Godhead as Father, Son, and Holy Spirit. God created humanity so He could love us and be loved by us.

The man and woman were perfect. They were sinless and knew nothing of evil, sickness, pain, heartache, or even death. God placed this couple in a perfect environment. It was weed-free and pest-free and immune to natural disasters such as hurricanes, tornadoes, earthquakes, and famine. There were no predators in this environment, and all the man and woman had to do was to care and tend the Garden—to harvest the unlimited and bountiful supply of food. Because of His deep and abiding love, God provided them with everything they needed to live full and happy lives. In return, God only desired their love and wanted this love to be shown through worship and obedience.

For love to be genuine, God created this first couple and all subsequent people with a free will—the ability to love or not to love, the ability to choose to do good or not to do good, the ability to obey God or not to obey God. God could have created people to love and to obey Him automatically, but then he would have created a race of robots, and people would not be capable of loving and worshiping God from their hearts. God gave this man and woman unconditional love, and love given freely in return is what He desires from all of us.

The only restriction God placed on this first couple was that they not eat the fruit of a certain tree. The tree was a test. By obeying God and not eating that fruit, they demonstrated their obedience to God.

Although this first couple was created without sin, evil had already entered the universe through the rebellion of the angel Lucifer. Lucifer was the most beautiful of God's creation. But Lucifer wanted more than anything else to usurp God, to become like the Most High. With a band of followers, he rebelled and was cast out of heaven. At that point in history, Lucifer became Satan (the Devil). It is important to realize that God did not create evil through Lucifer. Lucifer created evil by rebelling.

At an opportune time, Satan tempted the first couple with the same sin he himself had fallen victim to—a desire to be like God. With this promise, "You will be like God," Satan encouraged the first man and woman to disobey God by tasting of the forbidden fruit. Adam and Eve fell to this temptation.

As any parent knows, when children disobey, there must be consequences. Without consequences for wrong choices, especially when a warning was given in advance, free will loses its significance. The decision to sin loses it moral character, and there is no reason for children—or any of us—to stop sinning.

The consequences for Adam and Eve's sin was separation from God. Their banishment from the Garden of Eden is symbolic of this. They could no longer live in a protected environment free from weeds, predators, and natural disasters. Moreover, they had to toil for a living, and nature fought back with thorn and tooth and claw. Pain, suffering, and hardship became Adam and Eve's lot. Physical death would end their stay on earth. But worst of all, Adam and Eve lost their close fellowship with God; they became spiritually estranged from their Creator and in desperate need of a Savior to reconcile that relationship.

Adam was the corporate head of the human race. What does this mean? Simply that when Adam sinned, he represented all of us. Just as the decisions made by the ruler of a nation affect all the people subject to him, so Adam's decision to rebel against God affected all humanity. Like Adam, we too rebel against God and deserve punishment. In this sense we all share Adam's guilt.

Because Adam was representative of humanity, the Fall opened the door for Satan to have direct and powerful influence in this world system, including our individual lives. Satan effectively became the ruler of this present world, and humanity inherited a sin nature—a natural tendency to sin. Just as some diseases are passed on from generation to generation, so too sin is an inherited disease.

While Adam was created with a free will and could choose not to sin, today because of this sin nature, we are incapable of living sinless lives. As a result, sin is pervasive in every person, and it is out of this sin nature that we commit sinful acts. In short, the presence of evil in the world today can be laid upon Satan and humanity, not God.

Now, the idea that humanity is guilty because of something Adam did offends many people. They complain, Why should I be punished for something Adam did? But that's not the point. We are guilty for our *own* sins. People today, like Adam, are sinners, and we sin enough to deserve punishment on our own merits. Sin is real, and humanity sins corporately. The biblical account of the Fall is simply the historical explanation of how our tendency to sin came about and why there is suffering and evil in the world. No other religion or philosophy offers a better explanation.

But this is not the end of the story. The good news is, even before Adam rebelled, God, who knew that sin would enter the world, began to prepare a way for people to be healed from the effects of sin and to become reconciled to their Creator. God never loved Adam any less because of the Fall. And in spite of our sins, God never loves us any less. To demonstrate His love, God sent His Son to die on the cross to destroy the work and power of sin and to restore eternal fellowship with His creation.

The suffering and evil we see in the world today, then, is the direct consequences of our rejection of God. God wants us to love Him of our own free will, so He gave us the ability to choose to obey or to reject Him. Corporate humanity chose rebellion. Like any moral choice, there are consequences. God cannot tolerate sin in any form and had to respond with punishment. If He didn't, sin would lose its moral character, and there would be no reason for people *not* to sin. The consequences of sin play themselves out in evil and in suffering.

For Christians, the choices between good and evil are unambiguous. Sin is not relative, it is not dependent on human subjectivity, culture, or situations. Rather God has revealed very precise ethical practices and prohibitions in the Bible that are not open to human capriciousness or opinion. In this sense, ethics are absolute, and God is the absolute standard by which they are determined. Ethics are also unchanging and prescriptive; God expects people to behave according to His moral principles whether they wish to or not. Moreover, ethics are universal. They are applicable to all people and every culture, and they are the sole means by which one can judge and condemn evil.

In sum, the presence of evil and human suffering is in character with human nature and our sinful actions. God did not cause sin, but He does allow its natural consequences to follow human choices. This brings us to God's solution to the problem of evil.

Salvation and Eternal Life

In humanity's "fallen state," that is, in our rebellion against God, we are totally unable to reach out to God (Rom. 7:15–25; 8:7). This is understandable in part because our sin nature prevents us from measuring up to God's perfect and holy standard. No matter how hard we try, we always submit to sin (Rom. 3:23; 7:19), thereby continually breaking fellowship with God. It is impossible for people to earn salvation through their own efforts and good behavior.

In order for us to become reconciled with God, God Himself must take the initial step to achieve this reconciliation (and subsequently to open the door to salvation). God has done this in only one way. Out of His immeasurable love for people, God Himself came to earth as the incarnate Son, Jesus Christ, to reconcile humanity to Himself.

The Bible teaches that God wants everyone to enjoy eternity in heaven (1 Tim. 2:3–4; 2 Peter 3:9). Since people on their own initiative are unable to choose God and obey Him, God has provided us with a choice we *are capable* of making: accepting *by faith* Jesus Christ as our Lord and Savior.

The work of Christ here on earth is called the Atonement. Literally, the word means *to cover.* It involves the removal or covering of our sins by the substitutionary sacrifice of Jesus Christ on the cross (Rom. 5:8). Instead of guilty human beings making payment (redemption) for their sins, Jesus— God Himself—did it for us (Mark 10:45; 1 Cor. 6:20). This opens the door to reconciliation between God and humanity. Through Christ, we stand before God justified. On the basis of Christ's work, we are accounted righteous in God eyes (Rom. 3:23–24). Just as sin was charged to our account through Adam, so righteousness before God becomes ours when we accept this work of Christ in faith (Rom. 5:12–21). We are forgiven for our sins and our rebellion, and our relationship with God is restored.

A key point in this doctrine is that this forgiveness is not based on anything we do. We could never do enough good works to earn God's favor. Salvation is a free gift from God based solely on our acceptance of Jesus Christ as Lord and Savior (John 3:16; Acts 4:12; Eph. 2:8–9; Titus 3:5). To receive this free gift and the eternal benefits that go with it, we only have to invite Jesus into our lives, accepting Him and His work by faith (Rom. 10:9). The Christian message and hope are that simple.

By accepting Jesus Christ as our personal Lord and Savior, we immediately receive the blessings of three promises.

First, we receive eternal life (John 3:16; 14:1–4). This is the great hope of Christianity. Our earthly lives are temporary. We have a future life that will be free of pain and sorrow and where no evil will exist. Christians are pilgrims on this earth. With this promise and assurance from God, we face the daily sorrows and hardships of life. We even experience joy in spite of our sufferings. No other religion in the world can promise this hope and then back it up by the power of God's Spirit.

Second, God immediately begins to dwell with us (John 14:16–17). God does not promise He'll remove our hardships or make our lives more prosperous, but He does promise to lighten our loads (Matt. 11:28–30). And Jesus promises to dwell with us, even in this earthly life (28:20). Christians have the joy of daily communion with Christ and the prospect of continuous spiritual renewal and growth. We have a strength from outside ourselves that helps us endure our sufferings. No other religion in the world offers this.

Third, we are set free from the bondage of sin (Rom. 6:5–7). This is not to say that we will live sinless lives or live lives that are always pleasing to God (Rom. 3:23), but it does mean that we are no longer slaves to sin. Sin and evil can no longer have mastery over us, and we can draw closer to God and experience Him more fully as a result (Rom. 6:11–14).

The good news of Christianity is that Jesus died for our sins. Because of this, Christians enjoy restored fellowship with God. Rather than blame God for the evil and pain we experience, we rejoice in what He has done to remedy the problem of evil through His Son, Jesus Christ.

The Source of Truth

The legitimacy of any worldview is dependent upon its source of authority (and all worldviews, whether stated or not, have a source of authority, an explanation for why they believe as they do). If the source of authority is demonstrated to be unreliable, then the truth-claims arising out of that worldview have no standing. Without some form of verification, a religion's teachings on the nature of God and humanity, the origin of the cosmos, the source and remedy for human suffering and evil, and the path to salvation become groundless speculation—the words and thoughts of people, not God.

So if we wish to demonstrate that a religious worldview is erroneous, it is often more effective to attack its source of authority rather than its doctrines. Doctrines automatically crumble if the source of authority is proven to be inaccurate, contradictory, or contrived.

Verification of truth-claims must be relevant to the claims being made. For example, philosophical or other subjective claims must be internally and externally consistent and in harmony with reality as universally experienced. Factual claims must be verified by concrete evidence. In all cases, the source of truth must stand the test of objective scrutiny. Without a reliable and verifiable source of truth, there is no reason to accept any particular worldview over another—religious *or* secular.

The Christian Source of Truth

The basic presupposition of Christianity is the existence not only of a *natural* world but also of a *supernatural* world. The center of this supernatural world is God. He created us, and He created us for a purpose: to love us and to have us love, worship, and have fellowship with Him. This requires communication from God to His people—hence, revelation. Revelation is divine disclosure; it is God imparting information to people that could not be attained in any other way. For this revelation to be meaningful, that is, if it is to clearly reveal God and His plan and desires for humanity, it must be true. Thus to a Christian, divine revelation is the source of all truth.

Jesus is the clearest and most important revelation from God. He is truth (John 14:6). Jesus is God Himself. When on earth, He walked among people and He talked directly to them. But Jesus is not God's only revelation, nor, during the three short years of His ministry on earth, did He communicate everything God wants us to know. So God sent apostles to grant us additional revelation. However, like Jesus, the apostles walked this earth for a short time. Thus it is was necessary for both Jesus' and the apostles' teachings to be recorded and preserved. This is the purpose of the Bible.

The Bible, as the record of God's revelation, is the absolute source of truth on which the entire fabric of the Christian worldview rests. The Old and New Testaments, as originally inspired by the Holy Spirit and recorded by God's chosen writers, is seen as the complete, final, and inerrant revelation from God concerning Himself, the nature of humanity, the origin of the cosmos, the cause and cure of evil and human suffering, our eternal destiny, as well as all other matters concerning moral, social, and spiritual issues.

But How Do We Know It's True?

The evidence for the authenticity, reliability, and authority of the Bible is overwhelming. In fact, the Bible alone among the world's religious documents can verify its truth-claims with concrete, verifiable evidence. Demonstrating this, however, is an apologetic task that is beyond the scope of this book. Moreover, I have dealt with this subject elsewhere.[1] Nevertheless, I think it is important that I give a brief summary of the *kinds* of evidence available for study that clearly and specifically support the veracity of Scripture.

The first kind of evidence is *bibliographic*. This has to do with the question of whether the Bible we have today is close enough to the original writings to be equally reliable. The answer is yes. Scholars possess thousands of ancient manuscripts of the Bible, particularly of the New Testament. Some Old Testament manuscripts date back to the second century B.C. Scholars also possess New Testament manuscripts that date to within a few decades of their original writing. What does this prove? It conclusively demonstrates that existing copies of the Bible are almost word-for-word identical to the first manuscripts. Textual critics claim that today's Bible is 99.5 percent accurate to its original writings. This means that the Bible has not been corrupted, altered, or added to over the centuries of transmission. What God originally inspired is accurately recorded.

The second kind of evidence is *internal*. This evidence is particularly important to the historicity of Jesus Christ. The four Gospel accounts of Jesus' birth, life, ministry, death, and post-resurrection appearances were written by eyewitnesses to the events or by people who knew and interviewed the eyewitnesses. This is *primary source evidence*; it presents the highest level of validation available to historical events. What was recorded was actually witnessed by those who recorded it. New Testament historicity does not rest on oral tradition, hearsay, or circumstantial evidence.

The third kind of evidence is *external*. This is evidence from non-biblical sources. Other writers verify the historical accuracy of the Old and New Testaments by relating similar data. There is corroborating evidence from both Christians and non-Christians who lived close to the time the New Testament was written. These authors confirm, among other things, the authorship of the Gospels, the person of Christ, the birth of the Christian church, and other relevant facts recorded in the New Testament.

The fourth kind of evidence is *historical accuracy*. In every area in which the Bible can be checked out, it has been verified by non-biblical sources to be historically accurate. Its references to extinct nations and cultures, to ethical behavior and customs, to tools, weapons, and foods, to religious beliefs and practices, and to ancient kings and laws have been verified by archaeology. Nelson Glueck, a scholar who specialized in studying ancient documents remarked, "It can be stated categorically that no archaeological discovery has ever controverted a Biblical reference."[2]

The fifth kind of evidence is *prophetic accuracy*. Prophecy is an ingredient in many religions, including modern ones such as the Jehovah's Witnesses and Mormonism. Yet every non-Christian religion that touts prophecy has a long list of prophecies that have failed to come to pass as predicted. This is not the case with the Bible. Hundreds of biblical prophecies have come true. Every biblical prophecy concerning events up to the present time has come to pass.

The sixth kind of evidence is *scientific*. The Bible abounds in geological, biological, astronomical, meteorological, nutritional, and other data— most of the scientific processes for which were not understood at the time they were written (cf. Job 26:7; Isa. 40:22; Eccl. 1:6–7). All these descriptions are in total agreement with modern research.

In sum, the more the Bible is studied, the more the evidence mounts supporting its authenticity and reliability. Two facts surface relevant to this evidence.

First, if the Bible is truthful in areas where investigation can be applied, it is legitimate to believe that in areas of religious (spiritual) truth it is equally truthful and reliable.

Second, no other religious document in existence can offer the kinds of evidence used to verify the authenticity of the Bible. Other religions' truth-claims fall under one of three categories: (1) The babbling of false prophets who sometimes claim to have historical verification but cannot demonstrate it (human authority); (2) The fanciful philosophical writings and/or teachings of long dead (or living) religious "sages" with no credentials or confirmation at all for their authenticity (human reasoning); or (3) The subjective opinions of self-appointed gurus and other religious leaders who don't even try to verify their claims beyond private mystical experiences (human experiences). Only the Christian worldview has a source of authority (revelation) that stands the tests of historical, legal, and scientific verification.

If we are searching for religious truth, we are compelled by rational and objective evidence to consider as factual—absolute truth—the claims of Scripture. This will become even more apparent when we examine other major worldviews in the next five chapters.

CHAPTER EIGHT

Pantheism: All Is God

Every generation of Christians has had to confront heresies within the church—attempts to revise or change essential biblical doctrines from orthodoxy.[1] Likewise, Christians of every generation have had to defend their faith against the attacks of fraudulent religions from outside the church. Our generation is no exception.

The church today is battling one of its most powerful adversaries since the first century. This foe is particularly cunning because it not only attacks the church from without, but also from within. Most disciples of this movement practice their religion outside the church. However, others think of themselves as enlightened Christians and bring their beliefs into the church.[2] In either case, the historic understanding of essential Christian doctrine is reshaped and redefined to meld with their radical presuppositions.

For example, this view claims that Jesus is not the unique Son of God, but a mere man who somehow achieved "Christhood" by discovering his innate divinity. As a matter of fact, all people are divine—most just don't realize it. Moreover, sin is illusion or ignorance, not rebellion against a holy God. Spiritual truth is gained through mystical experiences or mediums rather than from divine revelation. The Bible is one of many "holy" books, not the unique, inerrant Word of God. Salvation can be earned by good works and progressive enlightenment, it's not a free gift from God through faith in Christ. Eternal life is unity with the god-essence, not spending eternity with God in a resurrected body.

You may have already guessed that I am referring here to the New Age Movement. Although the New Age Movement cannot be identified as a distinct religion because it entertains a variety of beliefs and practices (thus it's a movement rather than a sect), there is a central unifying motif. The theological point of reference for all followers of the New Age Movement is a pantheistic concept of God.

Pantheism is an Eastern philosophy that has been around for centuries. It is the theological mainstay of Hinduism, Taoism, some forms of Buddhism, and many Western religions, including Christian Science, Unity, Scientology, and theosophy.[3]

In our pluralistic society, traditionally Eastern religions are well-established faiths in the United States. However, many pantheists in this country do not identify themselves with a particular Eastern religion. Many probably don't even realize they're pantheists. Rather they belong to a loose coalition of religions, cults, and philosophical views that comprise a *westernized* form of pantheism tailored specifically to a secular worldview.

It is this ideology that we refer to as the New Age Movement, and its influence is widespread and rapidly growing throughout the United States. Most large secular bookstores dedicate whole sections solely to New Age books. Its philosophical presuppositions are common ingredients in movies, TV, cartoons, games, exercise programs, business and education seminars, health guides, martial arts programs, and the environmental movement. New Age philosophy is also tightly bound to postmodern thought.

Because of the immense influence of Eastern religious philosophy, it is worth noting how it became so popular in what has historically been a Christian country.

The Eastern Invasion

For more than a century, Eastern religious philosophy has been infiltrating the United States.[4] This escalated dramatically about thirty years ago. During the 1960s, the "counter-culture" movement began to reject traditional Western values, and America experienced major sociological upheavals. Secular humanism (which has been growing in influence since the eighteenth-century Enlightenment) moved onto center stage as the dominant worldview, and Christianity was shoved into the wings.

With Christianity losing its relevancy, Western culture began to experience a God-vacuum. People's intrinsic need for communion with deity was not being fulfilled by secular humanism. The time was ripe for a new religious movement, one that would embrace materialism and maintain the human-centered principles of secular humanism, while at the same time provide a "god" to fill the spiritual vacuum created by secular humanism.

For many Americans, Eastern pantheism molded to Western values became the answer. It provides a god to meet people's innate craving for a relationship with deity, but one who is non-threatening. This allows people to continue to focus on themselves, while God becomes an abstract and impersonal idea. This in turn means that sin is not rebellion against God, as Christians believe, and people are free to develop their own ethical standards. Amazing as it may seem, according to this religious view people themselves are divine, and everyone eventually will realize this. When this "truth" becomes well-known and accepted, the result will be heaven on earth: a "new age" of peace, prosperity, and global happiness.

There are three questions relevant to pantheism that need to be answered in this chapter: Can pantheists verify their truth claims? Does pantheism correspond to reality as universally understood and lived out? Does pantheism usurp Christianity as a more feasible worldview?

The answers to these questions will become clear as we compare Christianity's six worldview essentials outlined in chapter seven with their counterparts in pantheism.[5]

Although there are several varieties of pantheism, basic tenets can be identified as distinctive to its worldview. What follows is characteristic of the form of pantheism most popular in the West: pantheistic monism.[6] This understanding of deity forms the basis of Transcendental Meditation, Zen Buddhism, much of Hinduism, and New Age ideologies. Together, these four religious practices encompass the majority of pantheists in the West.

God

The most distinguishing feature of pantheism is its understanding of the nature of God. All other doctrines revolve around it and flow from it.

"Monism" is the concept that all reality consists of a single, impersonal substance or principle. In pantheistic monism, this impersonal substance or principle is God. God, then, is everything, and everything consists of God. He is all that exists, and nothing else exists but God. All of reality (the universe and everything within it) is God, and if something *appears* to exist that is not God, it is *maya* (an illusion) and really doesn't exist.

While Christians recognize that God is transcendent (He is separate from creation) and immanent (He is everywhere present and the sustaining force within creation), He is not identified as part of creation. Christians also understand that God is personal (we can have a one-on-one relationship with Him). Pantheists, on the other hand, identify God as part of creation and without personality. He is not a *He*, but more accurately an *It*. God is not a being to identify and worship as God. Everything is God.

One of the significance results of this view, and one that forever separates pantheism from Christianity, is that God is not sovereign over the lives of people. He does not intervene in human affairs through miracles and answered prayer. We are left alone to deal with the struggles of life and to work out our own salvation.

Humanity

What does this concept of God tell us about ourselves? For one thing, it tells us that we too are God. As the Hindus say, Atman (our true essence or soul) is Brahman (the essence or soul of the one Ultimate Reality—God).[7] In other words, if God is all there is to reality, then we too are part and parcel of God. Atman (our essence) is impersonal too. If we see ourselves as distinct personalities, it is *maya*—illusion. We are really one with God.

The goal of humanity is to recognize this. Our lives should be spent focusing on becoming united with God, not on the joys of living and serving God in the here and now. This is done by meditation and purging the body of all earthly cravings. We do not need to be concerned about our own welfare or, for that matter, the welfare of other people. After all, pain and suffering and material things are *maya*.

Here is an example of where the westernized form of pantheism parts company with Eastern pantheism. Westerners *are* concerned with pain, suffering, and material things. Hence, in the West, New Age pantheism does not necessarily stress an ascetic lifestyle.

Creation

If all is God, including the physical universe, then God is not a creator who exists apart from the universe He created. In pantheism, there is no separation of creator and created. While Christianity teaches that God created *ex nihilo*, that is, out of nothing (He spoke creation into existence), pantheists identify creation with God. Rather than *ex nihilo*, creation is *ex Deo* (out of God). Explained Geisler, "Creation springs out of God's being either by manifestation, emanation, or some kind of unfolding."[8] Some forms of pantheism see the physical universe as *maya*, and thus the created universe itself is nonexistent—it's illusion because only God exists. But pantheism in all forms maintains that the physical world is inseparable from God, and there is no creation as Christians understand it.

Suffering and Evil

If all is God, including both the spiritual and physical realm, then it follows that what appears to be human and animal suffering, as well as sin and evil, must arise from God's nature. This is exactly what pantheism teaches. However, to a pantheist God is not a moral being, and there is no distinction between good and evil in an absolute sense. The concept of oneness—that all is God—prevents this.

It is frequently stated that sin and evil are *maya* (illusion), and that for one to grasp that Atman is Brahman is to pass beyond good and evil. How can this be? Since Brahman is beyond good and evil, when people achieve oneness with God, when they unite with Him, they too move beyond good and evil. For most pantheists, sin and evil are illusions, the product of a lower level of existence that is dealt with through the law of karma (below).

Generally, pantheists stress the need to live moral lives. However, you can see that philosophically (and theologically) they have no basis for this teaching. Ethical behavior is reduced to relativism, and one's actions are amoral, that is they have no moral significance. One can be indifferent to moral standards and principles as well as to past, present, and future events.

Salvation and Eternal Life

Although the goal of all pantheists is to become united with God (Ultimate Reality or Brahman), there is no single way to achieve this: "There are many paths from maya to reality."[9] This means, of course, that salvation is *not* through Jesus Christ. Two processes are involved as one moves from the illusion of this life to oneness with Ultimate Reality: (1) the need to raise one's level of consciousness, and (2) the effects of the law of karma.

Consciousness. Mediation, chanting a mantra (sacred words repeated as an incantation), using hallucinatory drugs, and other techniques may be used to bring one to a higher ("altered") state of consciousness. This in turn brings one closer to unity with the Universal Reality (God). This process frequently involves rejecting (or denying) all material and physical cravings, or anything else that prevents one from progressing inwardly to unity with God.

It also involves a sacrifice of common sense. Accepting the God of pantheism is a step of faith that, unlike Christianity, moves us beyond the laws of logic and a rational understanding of reality. A Christian step of faith is always grounded on the objective truth of God's Word and most importantly on the historic resurrection of Jesus Christ. A pantheistic step of faith, on the other hand, requires that we reject the world of our senses. It's believing that what appears to be real is an illusion. Faith is emotionally accepting the premise that what looks and feels like reality is not real at all.

Law of karma. Until we reach oneness with God (or more accurately realize our oneness), our eternal souls are trapped in a seemingly endless cycle of illusionary births, lives, deaths, and rebirths as dictated by the law of karma. Karma is the principle of cause and effect that controls our destiny in reincarnation. It involves the retribution in later lives for sins committed in earlier lives. Depending on the sins committed, souls may be reborn into other human bodies or into insects or some other creatures. If our karma is steadily good, we will eventually free ourselves from the cycle of life and death and attain the higher level of consciousness that unites us with the all-encompassing God.

Ultimately, pantheists believe, everyone will reach oneness with God. However, this oneness is not a continuation of life in the Christian sense. There is no heaven populated by resurrected people. Rather heaven, if it can be called such, is absorption of the impersonal, eternal soul (Atman) into the Ultimate Reality (Brahman). Individual identity and personhood (which are really illusions anyway) vanish like a drop of water in the ocean. Existence as we know it (more accurately, imagined it) ceases—no one survives death in a resurrected physical body.

Source of Truth

While Christianity is a historic religion grounded in historic events, pantheism is wholly subjective. Unlike Christianity, there is no historical basis for belief. Ancient writings preserved in the Vedas are merely a record of the experiences and thoughts of Hindu sages with little insight into who wrote them or when. As a religious worldview, pantheism cannot be affirmed; its truth-claims cannot be verified.

To go a step further, pantheism is logically inconsistent because it violates the law of non-contradiction. To a pantheist, reality (what is real about the world) is beyond human knowledge and logic. As Geisler pointed out, "God is understood in the highest and most significant sense not by sensible observation nor by rational inference but by mystical intuition that goes beyond the law of noncontradiction."[10]

Let me share what Dennis McCallum observed about the illogical nature of pantheism (and other Eastern religions) in his recent book on postmodernism:

> Observers of religion are aware of a relativism that is part and parcel of Eastern mystical traditions such as Hinduism, Buddhism, and Taoism. These religions teach that everything is part of one essence, a belief system know as "monism" ("one"-ism). In Hinduism, the one divine essence is Brahman. In China it's the Tao, the Way. All these traditions reject reason as a tool for discovering truth. The central proposition of monism, that "everything is one," is no more rational than saying 1=1,000,000. They even utilize

contradiction to drive learners to a deeper or higher plane of understanding. Zen Buddhism, for instance, offers koans such as "What is the sound of one hand clapping?" The Hindu Brahman is "always and never." With its rejection of rationality, such paradoxical thinking is naturally compatible with postmodernism.[11]

A good example of this is the law of karma. On the one hand, pantheists claim that there is no such thing as sin, sin is *maya* or illusion. On the other hand, because of the law of karma, people are held accountable for their actions and punished for their sins. But if sins are illusions, why are people punished for them? To make matters worse, since these sins occurred in past lives, people are punished for sins beyond their control. It is hard to imagine a more unjust and illogical system.

Summary

Pantheism offers no verification for its truth-claims other than philosophical subjectivism—personal opinion. Pantheists themselves claim that God is unknowable and that one must go beyond human logic (whatever that means) in order to achieve oneness with God. We are expected to accept God based on human authority and personal feelings, not on divine revelation. Unlike Christianity, where faith is grounded in the objective truths of the Bible, pantheism requires a leap of faith that is carried to the ridiculous.

New Age Pantheism

In the beginning of this chapter, I noted that pantheism affronts the Christian church in two ways. First, externally, in the form of Eastern religions, such as Hinduism and Buddhism. These religions are well-established in the West and openly compete with the Christian worldview as distinct religions.

Second, pantheism affronts the church internally. I identified the vehicle of this incursion as the New Age Movement. It is not so much a religion, in the traditional sense of a group of people united by their commitment to specific doctrines and beliefs, as it is a philosophical ideal.

The New Age Movement is composed of numerous individuals and groups, often with diverse and even contradicting beliefs. They are united primarily by their adherence to pantheism—although a form of pantheism that is leavened with other religious and secular ideologies. Since this particular form of pantheism is the most active and influential variety here in the West, we will examine it more closely in the next few pages.

The New Age Movement is attracting both Christians and non-Christians by the tens of thousands and is rapidly infiltrating many churches and homes. Because followers of the New Age use words like *Christ consciousness* and traditional Christian symbols like the rainbow, and because they promote worthy activities such as environmental conservation and global peace, many Christians are fooled into believing that the New Age Movement is a Christian-like crusade that endorses Christian values. This is hardly the case.

New Age thinking aligns itself with pantheism by stressing the oneness of God, the divinity of humanity, relative ethics, an evolutionary concept of creation, and the belief that spiritual truth is subjective and experiential rather than objective and historical.

New Age pantheism, however, also maintains marked differences from its Eastern counterparts. In order for Christian evangelists to confront the New Age, these differences should be recognized. James W. Sire did an excellent job illuminating these differences. Let's see what he had to say:

> The New Age world view is highly syncretistic and eclectic. It borrows from every major world view. Though its weirder ramifications and its stranger dimensions come from Eastern pantheism and ancient animism, its connection with naturalism gives it a better chance to win converts [in the West] than purer Eastern mysticism.[12]

For example, unlike Eastern pantheism, but like naturalism (or secular humanism), the New Age Movement places greater emphasis on the value of people. Rather than seeing themselves as an insignificant part of the whole (a drop of water in the ocean of Brahman), followers of the New Age see individuals as important. As in Eastern pantheism, New Age believers seek to attain a higher level of consciousness in which they and the cosmos are one. But in the here and now, people are of value and are evolving to greater and greater heights of humanness. This will eventually result in a tremendous evolutionary transformation within humanity that will usher in a new age of prosperity, peace, and world order—a form of heaven on earth.

Second, New Age followers, like other pantheists, believe that reality consists of an immaterial (non-physical) universe accessible through *altered* states of consciousness. They also believe like naturalists (and secular humanists) that the physical universe is real and that it is accessible through *ordinary* consciousness.[13] This visible reality is under people's control, and people can create their own reality. This is not to say that the physical universe is an illusion.

Followers of the New Age, then, recognize two levels of reality rather than one: the immaterial reality entered into through altered states of conscious and the physical or visible reality controlled and created by the Self.

Third, New Age pantheism entertains a strong animistic bent. Animism is the original religion of primitive people worldwide. It is the belief that both good and bad spirits indwell organic and inorganic nature (trees, animals, rocks, lakes, lightning, mountains, and so on). Because the physical and spiritual worlds are inseparably bound together, these spirits are revered, feared, and manipulated to benefit people.

In a similar fashion, New Age adherents entertain a myriad of helpers (guides, guardians, or demigods) from the spirit world who instruct them and guide them into a deeper understanding of truth and reality.

Sire made this comment:

> They haunt the New Age and must be placated by rituals or controlled by incantations. The New Age has reopened a door closed since Christianity drove out the demons from the woods, desacralized the natural world and generally took a dim view of excessive interest in the affairs of Satan's kingdom of fallen angels. Now they are back, knocking on university dorm-rooms doors, sneaking around psychology laboratories and chilling the spines of Ouija players. Modern folk have fled from grandfather's clockwork universe to great-great-grandfather's chambers of gothic horrors.[14]

The New Age Movement is not new. It is simply the resurgence of ancient occultic practices and animistic religions mixed with humanism and Eastern pantheism (in particular, Hinduism) to form a religious recipe blended specifically to feed the spiritual hunger of Western secular people. In short, it is secular humanism with a cosmic ingredient. It maintains the humanist motto that "man is the measure of all things" and the humanist goals of global peace, prosperity, and unity, but to make humanism more spiritually palatable, it sugars it with "God."

Space prevents a complete rebuttal to all the doctrines outlined above, but a few observations will sound the death knell of both Eastern pantheism and its New Age counterpart.

Where's the Proof?

The most obvious problem with pantheism, especially when contrasted with Christianity, is its lack of historicity. It can't be validated. For example, Eastern and New Age religions claim that God is an impersonal force in the universe. But this is a meaningless statement. It cannot be affirmed *or* falsified by either self-evident propositions or by verifiable evidence. It's a truth-claim that cannot be checked out, so there is no way to demonstrate if it is true or false.

Pantheists try to skirt this problem by claiming that God is unknowable because He is above and beyond human logic. We can't intellectually comprehend God, they say. But this is nonsensical and self-defeating. Why? Because the very act of claiming that God is beyond logic is a logical statement about God. How can one make a logical statement about God if God is beyond logic?

Whether pantheism is true depends on whether you like what you hear. Contrast this position with Christianity.

Christians claim that Jesus "died for our sins according to the Scriptures, and that He was buried, and that He was raised on the third day according to the Scriptures" (1 Cor. 15:3–4). This claim can be examined. We can test it by investigating historical documents written by eye-witnesses (i.e., the Bible). We can research the authenticity and accuracy of the documents themselves to see if they stand up to critical scrutiny. Christianity encourages people to confirm its truth-claims (Acts 17:11).

An Illusive Illusion

The second major problem facing pantheism is more philosophical than historical. One of the essential truth-claims of Eastern pantheism is that there is no reality except the all-encompassing God. Everything else is illusion. But again, this is a nonsensical statement that is logically self-defeating. If everything is illusion, then those making that statement are themselves illusions. There's a real problem here. As Geisler pointed out, "One must exist in order to affirm that he does not exist."[15] When we claim that there is no reality except the all-encompassing God, we are proving just the opposite. The fact that we exist to make the claim demonstrates that there is a reality distinct from God, which makes this key doctrine of pantheism a self-defeating proposition. It is an untruth by definition.

Here's another way to see the same thing. It may be possible that nothing exists. However, it is impossible to demonstrate that nothing exists because to do so would be to deny our own existence. We must exist in order to affirm that reality doesn't exist. To claim that reality is an illusion is logically impossible because it also requires claiming that the claim itself is unreal—a self-defeating statement. If reality is an illusion, how do we know that pantheism isn't an illusion too?

In pantheism, people always behave as if they are dealing with reality—even if reality *is* illusion. If they break an arm, they hurt. If they get a fatal disease, they die. If they want food on the table, they work. So what's the point (or proof) of claiming everything is an illusion when we must live and act as if everything were reality? It doesn't make sense. Pantheists may pawn this inane philosophy, but no one can live it out consistently.

Pain and Evil Won't Go Away

Here is a third problem with pantheism. It is unable to account for human suffering and evil. Whereas Christians see the source of evil outside of God, they nevertheless recognize that God is sovereign and offers the solution to the problem of evil both in this life and in the life to come.

However, in pantheism God is not only unable to solve the problem of evil, He is the cause of it (remember, all *is* God). Pantheism and the New Age may try to ignore this problem by claiming that sin and suffering is illusion. But let's bring this philosophy down to the real world. Try to convince a man dying of cancer or a parent who has just lost a child that evil and suffering are illusion. Even if evil is an illusion, the illusion itself is real. In either case, evil exists. As Geisler asked, "If evil is not real, what is the origin of the illusion? Why has it been so persistent and why does it seem so real? . . . How can evil arise from God who is absolutely and necessarily good?"[16] The answer must be, if pantheism is true, God *cannot* be good, and He *must* be the source evil. There is no other way out of it.

Sin Is Sin by Any Other Name

This issue relates to a fourth problem inherent to pantheism. Because sin to many pantheists is an illusion, any attempt to distinguish between right and wrong is meaningless. If both good and evil flow from God, there is no criteria for ethical behavior. Ethics in pantheism must be relative; there is no absolute standard of right and wrong. Where does this take us? Carried to its logical conclusion, it results in moral anarchy because we are free to decide for ourselves what is morally right and wrong.

Some New Age followers try to outmaneuver this problem by claiming that sin is "an absence of knowledge." It is actions that occur out of ignorance. Once people realize their divine potential and get in tune with God's essence, and thereby achieve right information, the so-called sin issue will be remedied. To put it another way, since people are divine and thus innately good, once they recognize the severity of a problem, once they understand and become educated as to what is right and moral, they will make right decisions to correct that problem.

Here again we see the New Age pervasive denial of reality as everyone experiences it. We saw in chapter seven that humanity possesses a sin nature, a natural tendency to sin in spite of a desire not to do so. History and the real world confirm this. People smoke when they know smoking causes cancer. People steal when they know it's wrong. People eat fatty foods in spite of chronic heart problems. We have to teach our children to be good: by nature they lie, steal, cheat, and hit other children. The examples of our sin nature are endless. In the real world, it's obvious that people are not innately good. If they were, then our jails are so full of good people that there isn't enough room to hold them all!

Where Did I Come From?

Fifth, pantheism offers no explanation for the existence of life and the universe. In Christianity God transcends creation and thus is qualified to be the Creator. In pantheism, however, God can't be the creator because He is one in essence with creation—"It" is part of nature. Thus pantheism fails to answer one of humanity's most perplexing questions: the origin of life and the cosmos.

The Little God Who Can't Create

Finally there are tremendous difficulties facing the New Age doctrine that our essential nature is divine. As Sire pointed out, "We are confronted by indications of the opposite at every turn."[17]

Take, for example, the claim of many New Age followers that we can create our own reality. This should be possible if we are truly divine or part of God. Who has ever done it? Who has ever created a significant new reality that actually alters the status quo? I don't mean simply thinking oneself into a new job or curing a headache through so-called positive thinking. I mean creating a radically new reality. It's easy for New Age followers to claim this is possible, but if someone has ever done it, please step forward.

Look at it like this. If *you* could create reality, what would you create? Let me guess: growing younger rather than older; imagining an enemy out of existence; becoming rich on a five-dollar-an-hour job; having your favorite movie star fall head-over-heels in love with you; growing hair on a bald head; flying instead of walking; retiring tomorrow on Social Security; eliminating war; clearing out hospitals and orphanages; ending famine. I think you get my point. If you or I or anyone else could create reality, I suspect we would do more than just think ourselves into a fancy car or a better job or less arthritis. We would make significant and dramatic changes.

The whole idea that we can create our own reality just doesn't measure up to what we observe in the real world and how we live it out. We can claim that sickness is an illusion, but a broken arm still hurts, and people still die of diseases. We can say that morality is relative and that there is no distinction between right and wrong, but who really lives that way? I'm sure a New Age adherent will call the police as quickly as a Christian if a crook decides that his *personal* moral code allows him to rob the New Age adherent's home.

Will the Real Religion Please Stand Up?

Examples of our non-divinity are endless. This brings us back to the fact that it is one thing to make truth-claims, it is still another thing to prove them. All truth-claims are meaningless if they (1) do not adhere to the laws of logic, (2) do not correspond to reality and corporate human experience, and (3) cannot demonstrate their truthfulness to the highest level of certainty possible. Pantheism, then, is nonsensical because it (1) violates the laws of logic, (2) violates corporate human experience of what constitutes reality, and (3) cannot demonstrate that it's truth-claims are true.

CHAPTER NINE

What About Other Religions?

No book is exhaustive enough to cover every subject related to its field of inquiry. This is certainly true in the area of religion. I can't begin to analyze every religion and philosophy competing with Christianity. There are at least twelve hundred organized religions in America alone.[1] What I hope to adequately cover in this book are the religious and philosophical worldviews that the majority of Christians encounter at work, in the neighborhood, and among family and friends. But there are many others we could examine—some representing millions of devotees. Islam, for example, embraces many millions of devout followers worldwide. Between three- and four-million Muslims reside right here in the United States. Animism, the tribal religion of all primitive people, is still practiced in many parts of the world. There are also numerous cults vying for acceptance as purveyors of religious truth: Mormonism, Jehovah's Witnesses, Christian Science, The Children of God (The Family of Love), and Sun Myung Moon's Unification Church, just to name a few. Finally there is the occult: Satanism and witchcraft.

Even though space prevents an examination of these and other religions, the material presented in this book can still be useful as a guide for analyzing and testing their truth-claims. It can be applied equally well to *all* non-Christian worldviews.

Non-Christian religions simply do not have the kinds of objective evidence that supports Christian truth-claims. Most other religions do not even attempt to defend their beliefs. Let's return to Islam for a moment as an example. Although there are Islamic apologists, apparently many—if not most—Muslims do not engage in a rational defense of the Koran as Christians do the Bible. Their claim that the Koran is fully reliable as divine revelation is not based on "a critical examination of its veracity and historicity. They accept its truth by blind faith. They assume that neither God nor Muhammad would lie."[2]

Likewise tribal religions. Animists, such as the Native Americans in their pristine state, have no interest in rationally examining their truth-claims. Rather "faith in these systems is blind faith—reason cannot condemn or deny any aspect of their spirituality, according to adherents. Most tribal religious views are accepted from early childhood as part of what it means to be a member of the tribe."[3]

There is one issue relevant to the cults, however, that needs to be mentioned and briefly examined. It is the tendency of some cults to associate themselves with Christianity and, therefore, to claim that they reflect a more accurate revelation of the Christian worldview.

These cults promote a counterfeit Christian worldview. We must not confuse the cults with Christianity simply because cults use Christian terminology and claim to be Christian.[4] Think of all the cults as representing a single, distinct worldview—even though individual beliefs and practices vary from cult to cult. This can be done because all cults exhibit certain characteristics that set them apart from Christianity. We'll look at the most important.

What Is a Cult?

First, let's define what is meant by the word *cult*. According to Dr. Charles S. Braden, "A cult . . . is any religious group which differs significantly in some one or more respects as to belief or practice from those religious groups which are regarded as the normative expressions of religion in our total culture."[5] Historically in Western civilization, the "normative expression of religion" has been Christianity. Thus Christians identify a cult more precisely as a group "which surrounds a leader or a group of teachings which either denies or misinterprets essential biblical doctrine."[6] James Sire added this observation:

> Totally non-Christian movements like the International Society for Krishna Consciousness (Hare Krishna) and Transcendental Meditation (TM) are often not thought of as cults because they originate in another religious tradi-

tion. Still, their leaders often quote the Christian Scriptures as if they supported their own doctrine. So for this
reason, I will not emphasize their distinction from the
Christian-oriented cults.[7]

To Christians, a cult can be defined as a perversion of biblical Christianity.
A characteristic of many cults is their claim to be Christian or a *fuller*
revelation of Christianity.[8] This is what makes them so dangerous and why
I'm mentioning them in this book at all. Many Christians are seduced into
a cult by mistakenly believing that they represent just another Christian
denomination. And many non-Christians join a cult thinking they are becoming Christians. This confusion is made more hazardous because cults
frequently use Christian words and terminology, redefined to convey an
altogether different meaning than the Christian understanding. Thus a cult
member can speak of Christ, the Holy Spirit, faith, and sin but mean something entirely different from the orthodox Christian understanding.[9] This
is nowhere more evident than in Christian Science.

In her book *Science and Health With Key to the Scriptures,* founder
Mary Baker Eddy included a glossary of more than a hundred biblical
words whose meanings she presumptuously and unjustifiably altered. These
new definitions took on "spiritual" rather than literal meanings, which Eddy
declared better reflected their "original meaning."[10] For example, *Angels*:
"God's thoughts passing to man"[11]; *Baptism*: "Purification by Spirit; sub-
mergence in Spirit"[12]; *Death*: "An illusion, the lie of life in matter; the
unreal and untrue"[13]; *Father*: "Eternal Life; the one Mind; the divine Principle, commonly called God"[14]; *Jesus*: "The highest human corporeal concept of the divine idea"[15]; *Mother*: "God; divine and eternal Principle; Life,
Truth, and Love."[16]

Logic demands that only one among competing religions can reflect
divine revelation. They may *all* be false (including Christianity), but no
more than one can be right. This same logic applies to the cults. Regardless of whether a particular cult claims to be Christian or even agrees with
many Christian beliefs, if it does not adhere to essential Christian doctrines, it can't be Christian. This is exactly what all cults do. Here are a few
examples.

Jesus

The most significant departure from Christianity that all cults are guilty
of is rejecting Jesus Christ as God. No cult confesses Jesus as the Son of
God, the second person in the triune Godhead, eternally coequal in essence, power, and authority with the Father and the Holy Spirit. The Jesus

of the cults is far removed from the holy Son of God revealed in Scripture. Members of the Unification Church, for example, view Jesus as a man whom people not only can equal, but also can surpass. The Jehovah's Witnesses' Jesus is a unique, but still created, lesser god. To the Mormons, Jesus is the spirit brother of Lucifer. Christian Science speaks of Jesus as a human being who demonstrated "Christness" or the "divine idea," but He is not the resurrected Son of God.

Any person or religious organization that denies Jesus as the Son of God as revealed in the Bible is forever separated from Christianity (2 Cor. 11:4, 13; Gal. 1:8). All cults reject the Jesus of Scripture. On this evidence alone, no cult belongs in the Christian family. If Jesus is who He claims to be (fully God and fully human—1 John 2:22), the cults are wrong and are *not* Christian.

The Bible

Another area in which the cults deviate from Christianity concerns their view of Scripture. Most Christian cults claim to accept the Bible as authoritative, but not exclusively so, and only in accordance with their own interpretation. Observed Sire:

> Many cults claim to have a high regard for [Scripture]. Jehovah's Witnesses, for example, claim the Bible as their sole authority. The Mormons place it first in their list of Scriptures. The Unification Church of Sun Myung Moon also gives it an authoritative position, as does Mary Baker Eddy and Christian Science. Even the Maharishi Mahesh Yogi, founder of Transcendental Meditation, and other writers in the Eastern traditions quote favorably from the Bible.[17]

Their interpretations, of course, are based on their own presuppositions and religious views. Also, the major cults, such as Mormons, Jehovah's Witnesses, and Christian Scientists, have other "holy" books or writings that serve as an interpretive framework for the Bible. The cults reject both the inerrancy of Scripture as well as its singular and absolute authority.

Source of Authority

A third significant way in which the cults deviate from orthodox Christianity is their tendency to unite around and focus upon an individual or organization that becomes the ultimate source of authority. The authority and power held by these individuals is said to be supernatural in origin. Thus Mary Baker Eddy can claim that her interpretations of Scripture are the "absolute conclusions . . . [of] divine revelation, reason, and demonstration."[18]

Cult members are often fanatical in their loyalty—sometimes giving all of their money to the organization and even forsaking family and friends. The cults in turn demand complete obedience and submission, with the threat of damnation for failure to comply. Thus devotees frequently come under the complete control of their leaders in all areas of life.

Changes in Doctrine

A fourth characteristic of the cults that is quite different from Christianity is this. Doctrinal issues are frequently capricious and subject to change. Unlike Christianity, whose essential teachings are universal and absolute and have not been subject to modification among orthodox Christians through two millenniums, cultic doctrines change according to the need of the moment. New revelation freely supersedes old revelation. The Book of Mormon, for example, has "required almost four thousand alterations from its original publication in 1830."[19] Some of these alterations have been significant. Mormonism's rejection of polygamy and their more recent dispensation of religious equality to African Americans reflect major and far-reaching doctrinal changes.[20] Apparently, the gods of Mormonism (there are many of them) have a hard time making up their minds!

I have barely touched the surface concerning the heretical nature and teachings of the cults. Fortunately, there are hundreds of books and numerous counter-cult organizations that can supply an abundance of documented evidences refuting all aspects of cultic teachings.

Having made this important detour, we can now return to the primary concerns of this book.

CHAPTER TEN

Naturalism:
There Is No God

We are moving into new territory. Christianity, pantheism, and the cults, although clearly disputing each other with regard to fundamental beliefs and practices and especially in their understanding of the nature of God, nevertheless agree that deity exists. They acknowledge that there is more to reality than what we can see, hear, touch, taste, and feel—although their concepts of the supernatural vary widely.

But in the next two chapters, we will examine worldviews that reject the notion that any kind of God exists. Reality stops with the material universe; nature is all there is to reality; there is no truth beyond the five senses. Moreover, people are capable—at least potentially—of knowing all there is to know about reality.

It's important to understand that in spite of the fundamental difference between a theist and a non-theist, that is between one who accepts the existence of deity versus one who rejects the existence of deity, both crave answers to the same questions. People are people regardless of their worldviews, and all seek answers to life's great and perplexing questions: Who am I? Where did I come from? Why am I here? What happens after death?

When we approach the question of truth, we can use the same criteria for both a theist and non-theist. Atheists have the same questions about life and the cosmos as Christians; they just seek answers to them in the absence of God. To them, ultimate reality—what is real about the universe—is *natural* not *supernatural*.

This brings us to the worldview at hand: naturalism. Naturalism is the philosophical foundation of atheism. It's an attempt to satisfy the same deep psychological need for answers to life's perplexing questions that religion does. In this chapter, we will determine whether or not naturalism is any closer to truth than pantheism, the New Age, or the cults.

What Is Naturalism?

As a philosophical worldview, naturalism is Christianity's major competitor in the Western world. Naturalism is a highly influential and widely accepted philosophical system—and it is the antithesis of Christianity. In a world drifting from its religious moorings, the influence of naturalism on modern thought—even among theists—cannot be underestimated.

Naturalism is clearly the guiding light, *the* presupposition, underlying science, education, social structures, modern psychology, and just about every other field of human endeavor.

If Christians are to successfully share the Gospel in modern society, they must understand this prevailing mind-set, and they must be able to demonstrate the errors of its assumptions and conclusions. The following major tenets of naturalism are the same worldview ingredients we discussed both in Christianity and pantheism.

God

At a foundational level, naturalism is the direct opposite of theism in one fundamental way. For a theist, God dominates; for a naturalist, any concept of God is vigorously denied. Reality is composed only of matter—there is nothing but nature, and everything has a natural explanation. The universe itself is a closed system that has always existed—it's eternal. It operates like a gigantic machine according to unchanging natural laws. Nothing outside this closed system (the physical universe) exists.

Reality is what we can see, hear, touch, taste, and smell, and at least potentially all of reality can be understood by the human mind. There is no God who can interrupt natural laws or change the course of nature. There are no miracles, angels, providence, immortality, heaven, sin, salvation, and answered prayer. All such things are incompatible with naturalism's worldview.[1] Astronomer Carl Sagan summed it well: "The Cosmos is all that is or ever was or ever will be."[2]

Humanity

Since all of reality can be reduced to matter, humans are only physical beings. We are not created in the image of God, but are the products of mindless evolution. We are not body, soul, and spirit, as taught in the Bible (1 Thess. 5:23), but just body. Moreover, like the universe, we function like a machine—the laws of nature apply to us the same as they do to all other things. In fact, everything about us can be reduced to chemical and physical processes. Even our thoughts (our minds) are a product of chemical and neurological impulses.

In spite of viewing us as nothing more than atoms and molecules, most naturalists agree that human beings are distinct from other creatures. The fact that we can engage in conceptual thought and communicate these thoughts, maintain a sense of historical, cultural, and social connectedness, and possess a moral conscience indicates an elevated level of existence. Be this as it may, however, all naturalists still see Homo sapiens as the product of random evolution and think that all human traits can be accounted for through purely natural processes.

Creation
There is no creation. Matter is all there is, reality is the physical universe and its natural laws, and both have always existed.

Suffering and Evil
Suffering and evil, in the Christian sense of being the inevitable result of the Fall, are a myth. Ethics are relative and are not seen as absolute standards of right and wrong. Ethics are simply a projection of our subjective feelings and experiences—sometimes referred to as "corporate human consciousness." There is nothing outside of people by which to judge good and evil. Sin is synonymous with survival of the fittest: people seeking dominance over each other by whatever means possible. Only our sense of social order allows sin to be seen as sin at all. There is no theological basis for defining sin or for normative ethical behavior. If people instinctively know that murder is wrong, it is because this information was programmed into them through evolution for the sake of maintaining the human race, not because it is right or wrong according to God.

Salvation and Eternal Life
If people are only matter, without spirit or soul, and are governed by the same natural laws that govern all other entities in the universe, it follows that death is the end of existence. We neither arise after death in a new resurrected body (Christianity) nor merge with the great Absolute (pantheism). We simply cease to exist.

This is probably the most difficult doctrine for committed naturalists to accept. It is more than coincidental that the same period that witnessed the demise of the Christian worldview, due primarily to the acceptance of secular humanism (fueled by naturalism), also witnessed an unparalleled rise in Christian cults and New Age religions.

People instinctively recognize that there is more to life than the here and now and throughout history have believed in some form of afterlife (and hence God). Naturalism may reject the notion of the existence of God, but people haven't. As the influence of Christianity fades, people seek other gods to fill the spiritual vacuum created by naturalism. People haven't lost their craving for spiritual truth: they have just wandered from revelation to self-deception.

Source of Truth

Whether or not a particular worldview is an accurate expression of reality is determined by its source of truth. On what does a worldview base its truth-claims and assumptions? Is that source of truth verifiable? Verification, as we've seen, is the only objective and adequate test for the reliability of a worldview. The greater the quantity of and more varied the evidence supporting a particular worldview, the more trustworthy are its truth-claims and the more probable they are to reflect reality.

Naturalism has two primary sources of truth: philosophy and science. We'll look at both of them and see why they are *not* adequate sources of truth for confirming naturalism.

Philosophy

The philosophical argument supporting naturalism relates specifically to the question of God's existence. Does He exist or not? If God does not exist, then naturalism is reality. But if God *does* exist (I'm speaking here of the Christian concept of God), then all theistic beliefs (creation, miracles, answered prayer, providence, angels, afterlife) are logically justified. Why? Because if God exists, nothing is logically impossible for God so long as it doesn't violate His essential nature (e.g., God can't lie because He is by nature Truth). Philosophically if you are arguing for or against naturalism, you are actually arguing for or against the existence of God.

However, to sustain itself, naturalism must present confirming evidences, not talk philosophy (although there *are* philosophical arguments supporting the existence of God[3]). Naturalism makes specific claims about reality that must be verified if it is to be accepted. The foundation of naturalism may be a philosophical issue, that is, it begins with the question of whether or not God exists, but the proof of naturalism itself does not stem from philosophy. The argument of whether or not naturalism corresponds to reality must be solved by evidence. This evidence is scientific in nature.

Having said this, however, I need to point out that you cannot entirely separate science and philosophy. Much of science is motivated by and operates according to particular philosophical presuppositions that may or may not be correct. So although our concern here is whether or not science per se can adequately verify naturalism—whether or not it can sustain its truth-claims through evidence—we will nevertheless be dealing to a large degree with the philosophy of science.

Science

A word is appearing in books and journals with increasing frequency. This word is *scientism,* and it is used to convey the idea that ultimate truth comes from science. It logically follows that if the foundational motif of naturalism is true—God does not exist and all of reality is matter—science is the foremost dispenser of truth.

Philosopher of science J. P. Moreland defined scientism this way: it is the assumption that "only what can be known by science or quantified and tested empirically is true and rational."[4] In other words, he explained:

> Science is the very paradigm of truth and rationality. If something does not square with currently well-established scientific beliefs, if it is not within the domain of entities appropriate for scientific investigation, or if it is not amenable to scientific methodology, then it is not true or rational. Everything outside of science is a matter of mere belief and subjective opinion, of which rational assessment is impossible.[5]

This concept effectively equates reality with scientific truth. But notice something: The root of scientism is philosophy, not science. Observed Moreland: "The statement itself ['Only what can be know by science or quantified and tested empirically is true and rational'] is not a statement of science, but a second-order philosophical statement about science."[6] In fact, Moreland pointed out, it is a self-refuting statement because the "statement [itself] cannot be tested empirically, quantified, and so on."[7] In other words, at its very core, the essential claim of scientism is not scientific because it cannot be tested. It is a philosophical statement about science, not science itself.

This is why we cannot entirely separate science from philosophy. Science operates according to presuppositions that are philosophical in nature.

But let's look at claims of scientism more closely. Is there evidence to support its essential presupposition that science is the ultimate purveyor of truth? Naturalists think so, and if they are correct, theism is in big trouble.

Is All Truth Scientific?

Because we live in modern Western society, all of us are inadvertent victims of the philosophical assumption that science is the ultimate purveyor of truth. This claim is preached as a matter of fact by educators, in text books, in the media, and of course in all the sciences. We are programmed to accept scientific proof as the ultimate truth-test in whatever area it pronounces judgment—including religion (i.e., God does not exist). But as Philip Johnson pointed out:

> If the atheists make the rules, the atheists are surely going to win the game, regardless of what is true. The rules limit science to naturalistic theories and provide that the best available naturalistic theory can be considered successful even when it rests on unverifiable assumptions and conflicts with some of the evidence.[8]

The view that science provides the ultimate truth-test is a myth. To begin with, science is limited in what it can investigate, where it is applicable, and what truths it can discover. Let me explain.

There are many avenues of truth that lie outside the scope of science. According to the *Oxford Dictionary,* science "must involve proof and certainty, must not depart from what can be generated rigorously from immediate observation, and *must not speculate beyond presently observable processes"* [emphasis added].[9]

Science has no bearing on historical, legal, philosophical, theological, or aesthetic issues and should not even speculate in these fields. When it does, it is dabbling in areas of truth for which it is not qualified to investigate or to pronounce judgment. Can science prove or disprove that George Washington was our first president (historical truth)? Can science prove or disprove that a murder was premeditated (legal truth)? Can science prove or disprove the validity of the presuppositions people bring to ethical issues (philosophical truth)? Can science prove or disprove the existence of God (theological truth)? Can science tell us if a book was good or a piece of art beautiful (aesthetic truth)?

In all these cases, science has nothing to say (or shouldn't, if it wishes to maintain its integrity). Why? Because science derives its knowledge through observation (if not directly at least indirectly) and experimentation—the world of sense perception. Scientific laws and theories are verified by their repeatability and dependability, and this is determined by continued research, experimentation, and observation. There are many areas of knowledge not subject to scientific investigation and verification.

Let me add quickly that I am not talking here about the scientific method or the scientific approach to acquiring truth as described in chapters five and six. I'm speaking specifically about applying the conclusions of science or extrapolating the philosophy of science (naturalism) to other fields of knowledge. As we saw, the scientific approach to discovering truth is valid in other areas of knowledge besides science. But taking the findings of science or applying the presuppositions of science to non-scientific issues in order to determine truth in other fields of knowledge is both irrational and erroneous. You cannot use a philosophy which by definition denies the existence of God (naturalism) to prove God does not exist. This is stepping beyond the bounds of rational argumentation and employing circular reasoning. Other evidence that is not prejudiced by naturalism must be considered.

To be fair, the same can be said about theism. One cannot rely entirely on theistic presuppositions to demonstrate that God exists—not if you wish to be effective in evangelism. This too would be begging the question. This is why apologetic evangelism encourages the use of nonbiblical evidences and the scientific method of inquiry in order to get a fair hearing on theological issues.

Most unbelievers will walk away shaking their heads if we try to prove God's existence simply by reading Genesis chapter one. If they have already rejected the Bible as Hebrew mythology and creation as religious dogma, why should they believe in a God whose existence is demonstrated only in Scripture? To get a fair hearing, we either have to confirm the authenticity and reliability of the Bible, therefore proving it's an accurate revelation of God, or we must present other, nonbiblical, evidences for His existence.

Science and Christianity

What I'm moving toward is this: Science is not the Great Absolute, the ultimate source of truth and knowledge. This is so for two reasons: (1) science is limited in its field of inquiry and cannot pass judgment in any non-scientific area of truth, and (2) science operates within its own philosophical worldview, its own biases, and it depends on philosophical presuppositions that may or may not be accurate—like any other worldview. If these assumptions are inaccurate, then the truth-claims that arise out of them and depend upon them are erroneous.

This brings us to the conflict between science and religion, in particular, between naturalism and the Christian worldview.

Contrary to the claims of naturalists—who flat out deny any religious truth—when an apparent contradiction arises between science and Christianity, it does not always result in victory for science and defeat for Christianity. Science has nothing to say about theological issues. Science can't disprove the existence of God any more than it can disprove any other theological truth-claim. Science can't refute the reality of answered prayer, the existence of angels, or the absolute nature of Christian ethics.

But how about the opposite? Can theological truth refute scientific truth? Yes. Christian truth-claims, if adequately substantiated, *can* modify or even refute scientific truth-claims. This may be a shocking statement, immersed as we are in the philosophy of scientism, so let me carefully explain what I mean.

Consider the well-known fact that many so-called scientific theories have ultimately, with the passage of time and with additional research and evidence, been proven to be incorrect. The history of science abounds with examples of discarded theories.[10] On the other hand, biblical truths are absolute and final. Which should be the most trustworthy?

Look at it like this. Science cannot alter or change history because historical facts are past events and unalterable. So whatever *actually* happened in history must be true. On the other hand, science is in a constant state of flux because it deals with the here and now and is dependent upon continuing research, observation, and experimentation. Its truth-claims, by their very nature, are less reliable than historical facts because new evidence can always surface to alter existing concepts. In sum, if the two kinds of evidences confront each other, the strongest will always be historical because it is unchanging while scientific evidence is subject to modification.

This may seem like comparing apples with oranges. You may think that comparing historical evidence with scientific evidence is meaningless because they are concerned with entirely different kinds of truth. Not necessarily so. There are times when science forces us to make this comparison and to decide which evidence is most valid.

Scientific claims are sometimes used by naturalists to discredit biblical truths when the evidence supporting the biblical view presents a stronger argument than the evidence supporting the scientific view. When this happens, one is forced to go with the best evidence—that which can better verify its claims—even if the evidence is religious or historical rather than scientific. Let me illustrate this with two examples: naturalism's rejection of miracles and creation.

Miracles. Naturalism rejects the notion of miracles—supernatural events outside the domain of natural laws. It rejects them on philosophical grounds—miracles fly in the face of naturalism's anti-supernatural bias. The Bible, on the other hand, is replete with miracles. Who's right? Since naturalism states that *all* miracles are impossible, it only takes one miracle to disprove naturalism in this area. So let's take the Bible's most celebrated miracle, the resurrection of Jesus Christ.

Almost everyone today, including atheistic scholars, agree that Jesus is a historical person. The primary (but not the only) source of information about Jesus is the Bible. On the basis of accepted principles of textual and historical analysis, the biblical accounts of Jesus' life (the Gospels) are found to be trustworthy historical documents—primary source evidence for the life of Christ.[11] In these records, Jesus claimed to be God in human flesh and predicted that He would die and rise again on the third day to prove this claim (Matt. 16:21; Mark 8:31; Luke 9:22; John 2:19–21). His death and post-resurrection appearances are confirmed by eyewitnesses and recorded in historical documents (the Gospels).

Jesus' resurrection, then, is a historical event confirmed by overwhelming historical testimony, the same kind of testimony used to validate other historical events. Moreover, the resurrection of Jesus Christ is irrefutable by science. Why? Because science operates in the here and now and can't disprove any historical event—such events are beyond scientific inquiry. The truthfulness of all miracles must be determined by avenues of evidence other than science, namely historical evidence.

So what can we conclude? Since the resurrection of Jesus Christ is clearly demonstrated as factual by all the canons of historical investigation, and since science's claim that it is a non-event is supported only by its anti-supernatural presupposition, we must go with the best (the historical) evidence. The conclusion is that the Resurrection (and thus at least one miracle) occurred.

Here we have a case—and one of dozens we could examine—where a claim of naturalism is overshadowed evidentially by a claim of Christianity. The honest inquirer will concede that miracles are a fact of history, and naturalism is unable, evidentially, to dispute that fact. In short, the naturalist's denial of the Resurrection is based solely on their commitment to philosophical naturalism—at the expense of "irresponsible handling of the historical evidence of Jesus."[12]

Creation. Let me offer an example straight from science. Naturalists zealously adhere to an evolutionary origin of life. Indeed, naturalism stands or falls on whether or not life and the cosmos arose from random natural process rather than from God. On the other hand, the Bible says, "In the beginning God created the heavens and the earth" (Gen. 1:1). What should we believe?

We have the same scenario as we did with the issue of miracles. We have a document (the Bible) of proven reliability. In every area in which it can be checked out—including scientific claims—the Bible has been veri-fied as accurate and truthful. Does evolution have this same track record? Not at all. In fact, no one has ever presented a workable, let alone prov-able, evolutionary model that all scientists agree with or that can be sub-stantiated by reliable scientific evidence. And remember, science can only work in the here and now. The origin of life was a historical event. Many evolutionists admit that old-fashioned Darwinian evolution is no longer a viable model of origins.[13]

If the Bible says that *creation* is a fact (and if there is overwhelming evidence that the Bible is a truthful document), and if naturalism says *evo-lution* is a fact, but fails to present adequate evidence to support this claim, who are we to believe? Which view has the preponderance of evidence to support its view? Unquestionably, it is the Bible. The evidence supporting the Bible is much greater than the evidence supporting naturalistic evolution. We are therefore justified in trusting the Bible over unsubstantiated scien-tific claims—especially when these claims deal with areas outside the realm of science and stem from anti-supernatural presuppositions.

More than Scripture. The evidence for creation is not dependent on just the historical reliability and veracity of Scripture. Creationism stands the test of critical scrutiny on scientific grounds as well. Creationism—the premise that God was actively involved throughout the creation process—is consistent not only with Scripture but with the very data evolution has a difficult time accounting for. Here are a few examples.

The various evolutionary theories are unable to explain (though they try) why there is no fossil evidence of transitional species ("missing links" between two kinds of animals, such as amphibians and reptiles). Creation-ists point out that there are no transitional fossils between groups of ani-mals because God created living creatures "after their kind" (Gen. 1:24). In other words, God created amphibians, reptiles, birds, and mammals as specific animal types, and it is from these original "kinds" of animals that the great varieties of extinct and existing animals arose. But these crea-tures did not evolve from one species into another—there is no concrete evidence for this.

A second obstacle for evolutionists that is not a problem to creationists concerns mutations. Evolutionists argue that the mechanism by which one species evolves into another is through genetic mutations. There are two problems with this. First, in practically every known case, a mutation is not beneficial but harmful to an animal and usually kills it. A deformity lessens the survival potential of an animal—it does not strengthen it. Sec-ond, even if the earth is five and a half billion years old, as evolutionists claim, there is still not enough time for even a simple organism to evolve into a more complex organism through random mutational changes. The time needed is many billions of years longer than the age of the universe itself, even if the universe is as old as science estimates.[14]

Other problems with evolution include the Laws of Thermodynamics, which imply that the universe is both finite and had a Creator. The First Law states that matter and energy are neither being created nor destroyed. In other words, matter and energy do not have within themselves the ability to create. This implies that matter must have been created. The Second Law states that entropy (which is the measurement of disorganization) always increases in an isolated system (a system which does not have an external influence that can sustain or increase its available energy, such as the universe). Now, what does this mean? Simply that the natural tendency of things is to wear out and grow old (old automobiles rust away; you and I grow old and die). But if the universe is running down, it must have had a beginning. It is not eternal; it had a Creator.

There are numerous other problems inherent in the theory of evolution that are perfectly explained in a creation model of origins.

We are justified to reject evolution on biblical grounds alone: the Bible is demonstrated to be reliable, and evolution is fraught with difficulties. But we also have scientific evidence that clearly supports Creation. The case for Creation is twofold: the testimony of Scripture and the testimony of science.

The Real Problem

I cannot emphasize enough that when contrary opinions surface between science and Christianity, it is usually because science has moved beyond its field of inquiry and into the philosophical or religious arena. Consequently, it is not only legitimate but wise, when analyzing scientific claims that attempt to thwart the Christian worldview, to consider all the evidence, including nonscientific evidence.

Remember, scientism rigorously adheres to the philosophy that data must meet scientific standards of inquiry and validation or it can't represent truth. But this is a presupposition—an assumption flowing out of naturalism's anti-supernatural worldview. Assumptions don't automatically equal truth. They may or may not be correct. It is very unscientific for science to ignore valid evidence just because it is non-scientific in nature. Science can't brush aside appeals to other avenues of truth just because they don't fit in the scientific paradigm of how truth should be determined.

This is not to say that Christians can ignore scientific evidence, but it is to say that nonscientific evidences can be brought to bear on many issues. Scientism errs both philosophically and logically when it attempts to belittle such evidence by off-handedly claiming it cannot represent truth simply because it is religious and not scientific.

J. P. Moreland explained this concept well and is worth quoting at length:

> Larry Laudan [in his book *Progress and Its Problems*] has argued that the history of science illustrates that conceptual difficulties from philosophy, theology, logic and mathematics, political theory, and general worldview considerations provide negative evidence for the rational acceptance of scientific theories in the form of external conceptual problems. "Thus," he says, "contrary to common belief, it can be rational to raise philosophical and religious objections against a particular theory or research tradition, if the latter runs counter to a well-established part of our general *Weltbild*—even if that *Weltbild* is not 'scientific' (in the usual sense of the word)."
>
> This observation makes sense. If science really is not an isolated discipline tucked away in an airtight compartment, if one has good arguments or reasons for holding to some proposition, and if a scientific theory conflicts with that proposition and is not merely complementary to it, then the proposition itself provides some evidence against the scientific theory. This is so even when the proposition in question is theological, philosophical, or related to some other discipline outside science. The real issue is not what kind of proposition it is, but how strong the evidence is for it.
>
> Anyone wanting an integrated world view will see that nonscientific problems, if they are rationally supportable, will count against conflicting (though not complementary) scientific claims; thus, such external problems should be used in assessing those scientific claims. Put another way, by its very nature, science interacts and sometimes conflicts with other rational fields of study. Thus, it's not inappropriate to the nature of science or to the way science has been practiced through history to raise theological or philosophical considerations as part of the assessment of a scientific theory, if those considerations are rationally justifiable on their own grounds.[15]

A Word of Caution

This too needs to be said. Christians should not make every issue a theological one, nor should they seek to justify every issue according to whether or not it conforms with Scripture. Doing this will frequently result in a failure to get a fair hearing from the scientific and non-Christian communities.

In the Creation versus evolution debate, for instance, even if Christians are justified in rejecting evolution on the weight of Scripture alone (because the Bible sustains more and wider verification than the theory of evolution), it is a grave mistake to point to Genesis as the sole evidence for creationism—not when there is a wealth of scientific evidence supporting creationism that can be brought to bear on the discussion. This is why I pointed out that creationism can be sustained by scientific evidence as well as biblical evidence.

Christian apologists must be sensitive to where unbelievers are coming from and seek a point of contact from which unbelievers will listen. If an unbeliever enters into a discussion on evolution already convinced that the biblical account of creation is Hebrew mythology, then Christians should present scientific evidence to support the Christian view. As the apostle Paul said, we must become "all things to all men, that [we] may by all means save some" (1 Cor. 9:22).

What Have We Seen So Far?

Scientism is the source of truth for naturalism. Or to put it another way, for a naturalist, truth comes only from science. It should be clear by now, however, that this attitude is narrow-minded, prejudiced, and designed to preclude any source of truth that does not pass through naturalism's anti-supernatural grid.

We have seen repeatedly that in order for a worldview to be acceptable, it must be both internally and externally consistent and it must correspond to reality as is universally understood and lived out. Naturalism not only fails to recognize the value of spiritual truth, but it refuses to consider its existence. It does this for a very good reason—survival. If God exists, naturalism as a worldview crumbles.

The Christian worldview recognizes the existence of both a natural *and* a supernatural realm. It understands that spiritual truth is a product of the supernatural realm. This conviction is internally consistent (obedient to the laws of logic), externally consistent (as evidences for creation and miracles illustrate), and it corresponds to reality as universally understood and lived out (lives are changed through the Christian experience).

On the other hand, naturalism exhibits insurmountable difficulties. Internally, it refuses to recognize the logical possibility of the supernatural because it builds its worldview on an unyielding anti-supernatural presupposition. Externally, it fails to account for (or admit to) the overwhelming objective evidences confirming supernatural realities, such as historical evidence for miracles and fulfilled prophecy. Finally naturalism fails to correspond to reality as universally understood and lived out because it refuses to acknowledge as real the world-wide phenomenon of spiritual fulfillment and the role such fulfillment plays in subjective human experiences. To naturalists, spiritual fulfillment is psychological, a product of the human imagination. To Christians, spiritual fulfillment is a profound peace of mind and a dramatic change in worldview flowing from a personal relationship with the living God.

What can we conclude from this? If the foundation of an edifice is knocked down, the structure resting on it is destroyed. This is the case with naturalism. Naturalism is not only unable to disprove the existence of God and other spiritual realities, it doesn't even have the resources to attempt to disprove them. Spiritual truth lies beyond the scope of science. Scientism is not, and cannot be, the source of all truth.

CHAPTER ELEVEN

Secular Humanism: Man Is God

We have examined two ways in which the Christian worldview is under attack in modern Western society: pantheism and naturalism. In the first instance, God is an impersonal entity that permeates all things and encompasses all things. Some pantheists believe that people by virtue of their "oneness" with God are innately divine. This popular form of pantheism is the trademark of the New Age Movement. It's a view adapted to a secular worldview and distinct in several ways from its Eastern progenitor.

The second avenue through which Christianity comes under attack is naturalism. This particular view of reality is even more influential in the West than pantheism. Naturalism teaches that there is no God and that the material universe and its natural laws are all there is to reality.

The philosophy of naturalism is expressed as a distinct worldview in secular humanism. It is the philosophical foundation of secular humanism— it's what makes secular humanism work. As James Sire put it, secular humanism is "naturalism in practice."[1]

Like all worldviews, secular humanism is the filter through which its adherents interpret data, determine truth, and set values. In modern Western society, secular humanism, flowing from the philosophy of naturalism, is the prevailing worldview. It's *the* force shaping modern society. Even people who do not accept the anti-God presupposition of naturalism live lives that reflect this particular worldview.

Of course this doesn't automatically mean that secular humanism represents truth. So we pose the same questions to secular humanism that we did to pantheism, the New Age, the cults, and naturalism: Is secular humanism closer to the truth than any other worldview? Does it correspond to reality more accurately than Christianity? We will begin to answer these questions by clearly defining what secular humanism is.

What Is Secular Humanism?

The concept of humanism is not necessarily bad. It's simply a philosophy that puts special emphasis on the value of human beings. This is not unbiblical. People are created in the image of God (Gen. 1:27), and as such we *are* of value. The Bible clearly teaches that people are of much greater value than the rest of creation (Ps. 8; Luke 12:6–7).

Christians, while recognizing the value of corporate humanity and individual worth, do so in the full knowledge that this is due to our being created in the image of God and our being loved by God. Whatever value we possess comes from God and can't exist independent of Him. God is the ultimate good in the universe—not people. He is sovereign Lord over humanity, and people are accountable and responsible to Him.

The key ingredient of *secular* humanism, however, is naturalism, and naturalism is atheistic because it denies the existence of God. Thus *secular* humanism, by definition, is also atheistic. As professor Harold Berry pointed out, "A vast difference exists between humanism that is theistic and secular humanism that is nontheistic or atheistic."[2] It is one thing to recognize our worth as the crown of God's creation, and quite another to adhere to a philosophy that elevates humanity above God or denies that God exists—as in the case of secular humanism. In this chapter, when I use the word *humanism,* I'm referring specifically to atheistic *secular* humanism.

Secular humanists, by virtue of adhering to the evolutionary philosophy of naturalism, see human beings as the ultimate value in the universe. There is no sovereign, creator God who upholds and governs all things according to His will. Human beings are the pinnacle of evolution. We alone are self-aware and capable of ethical behavior. The human mind is master of the universe, or at least potentially so, and all knowledge is within our grasp. With this power, *we* control our destiny; *we* create our ethics; *we* write our laws; *we* determine all social and cultural behavior; *we* are autonomous and self-sufficient. In short: "Man is the measure of all things."

A State Religion

Secular humanism is the prevailing religious belief in Western culture. You may wonder why I refer to secular humanism as a religion. Technically that's precisely what it is. Webster's dictionary defines religion as "(1) a set of beliefs concerning the cause, nature, and purpose of the universe . . . often containing a moral code for the conduct of human affairs. (2) A specific fundamental set of beliefs and practices generally agreed upon by a number of persons or sects." The secular-humanist worldview provides its own answers to the cause, nature, and purpose of the universe as well as distinct moral codes. It is a set of beliefs and practices followed by the majority of people in the West. Hence, secular humanism is a religion.

There are other reasons for identifying secular humanism as a religion. Humanism's holy writ, the *Humanist Manifesto I*, refers to itself as "religious humanism." Even the U.S. Supreme Court recognizes this definition. In the 1961 case *Torcaso v. Watkins,* the Supreme Court declared that "among *religions* in this country which do not teach what would generally be consider a belief in God are Buddhism, Taoism, Ethical Culture, *secular humanism,* and others."[3]

For all practical purposes, secular humanism is the state religion of the United States. It is fully endorsed and promulgated by the United States government and our judicial system. Francis Schaeffer observed:

> The humanist world view includes many thousands of adherents and today controls the consensus in society, much of the media, much of what is taught in our schools, and much of the arbitrary law being produced by the various departments of government.[4]

Examples of this are innumerable. Federal funds are given to secular humanist activities that are diametrically opposed to Christian values: grants to universities that promote naturalistic concepts of education, science, psychology, and sociology; Planned Parenthood, which promotes abortion; the National Endowment to the Arts, which awards grants worth thousands of dollars to what many Christians consider pornographic and blasphemous art projects; and public school systems, where humanistic values are taught through sex education, value clarification, and naturalistic evolution.

Furthermore, laws are enacted on federal and state levels that mandate the acceptance of abortion, homosexuality, and other anti-Christian—but humanistic—values and behaviors. Schaeffer also noted:

> Law in this country has become situational law. . . . That is, a small group of people decide arbitrarily what, from their viewpoint, is for the good of society at that precise

moment and they make it law, binding the whole society by their personal arbitrary decisions. . . .

The law, and especially the courts, is the *vehicle to force* this total humanistic way of thinking upon the entire population. This is what has happened. The abortion law is a perfect example. The Supreme Court abortion ruling invalidated abortion laws in all fifty states, even though it seems clear that in 1973 the majority of Americans were against abortion. It did not matter. The Supreme Court arbitrarily ruled that abortion was legal, and overnight they overthrew the state laws and forced onto American thinking not only that abortion was legal, but that it was ethical.[5]

This same kind of governmental endorsement is being sought by the gay community. Homosexuals not only want the right to practice their sexual behavior in private and to be free from persecution for their lifestyles, but they want legislative endorsements that "fully legitimize homosexuality as an acceptable and sanctioned alternative lifestyle."[6] They want the world to believe that "gay is as acceptable as straight."[7] The gay agenda seeks "to codify their behavior as acceptable and good, to force their lifestyle on the rest of society, and to influence those too young to understand the moral implications of this issue.[8]

A Brave New World?

Is the world better off today under this prevailing religious climate? Let me again quote Francis Schaeffer:

The humanists push for "freedom," but having no Christian consensus to contain it, that "freedom" leads to chaos or to slavery under the state (or under an elite). Humanism, with its lack of any final base for values or law, always leads to chaos. It then naturally leads to some form of authoritarianism to control the chaos. Having produced the sickness, humanism gives more of the same kind of medicine for a cure. With its mistaken concept of final reality [naturalism], it has no intrinsic reason to be interested in the individual, the human being. Its natural interest is the two collectives: the state and society.[9]

Let me sum this up. The ethics and lifestyle promoted by secular humanism are being foisted upon all of us through our court system, through federal and state legislatures, through special interest groups, and through our educational system. Leading scientists and educators are the priests of "religious" humanism, and virtually the entire country is their congregation. Furthermore, because secular humanism (like many religions) is intolerant of competing religions, it ardently opposes Christianity. As Professor Harvey Cox wrote, "Secular humanism actively rejects, excludes and attempts to eliminate traditional theism from meaningful participation in the American culture."[10]

Because its chief supporters are the educational elite and those in control of the media, secularism human continually imposes its ideology on the American public. Wrote Steve Hallman, former vice president of the American Family Association:

> The rapid spread of humanist ethics owes much to positive, sympathetic treatment by the entertainment media in recent years. Television has shaped and molded many of our ideas ["By the time a child finishes high school, he has spent some 15,000 hours in front of T.V.—more time than in school"[11]]. And since television appeals mainly to the emotional rather than the rational, it can be a tremendous instrument of Change. Humanists have found that television makes a wonderful pulpit for the preaching of humanist ethics.[12]

Thus, Carl Sagan can declare as scientific fact on national television before 140 million viewers that "the cosmos is all that is, or ever was, or ever will be," and his poison is swallowed hook, line, and sinker by the unaware and uninformed. Reality is only what we can see, hear, feel, smell, and taste. Reality is naturalism, and flowing directly from it, secular humanism is truth.

How did we get to the point where an undeclared state religion dictates governmental policy and funding? The answer begins with the rejection of the Christian worldview.

In the Beginning

The story of how atheistic secular humanism came to replace Christianity as the principal worldview in Western society after fifteen centuries of Christian dominance is a story worth hearing. It not only explains the present state of affairs (the dominance of secular humanism), but it is a narrative analogous to the fall of humanity itself. It is the tale told afresh of Satan's age-old temptation to Eve that "you shall be like God"; it is the story of humanity turning from God and placing itself upon His throne of sovereignty, autonomy, and authority.

The Renaissance

The Christian worldview went generally unchallenged from the early fourth century through the Middle Ages. However, beginning in the Renaissance (the fourteenth to seventeenth centuries), a growing interest in Greek philosophy and science began to draw people's attention away from religious matters toward people and human interests. Church historian Harold Lindsell described it:

> [The Renaissance] taught man an opposite view of the world from that which had prevailed in antiquity and the Middle Ages. In place of a world looked at through the eyeglasses of a spiritual, religious, and poetic view it substituted a scientific, realistic, economic view. Abruptly humanity rejected that which it had hitherto allowed to guide it.[13]

Human reasoning began to dominate divine revelation. Renaissance philosophers such as Baruch Spinoza (1632–77) introduced the seeds of biblical criticism and rationalism, while Nicolas Copernicus (1473–1543), Galileo Galilei (1564–1642), and other Renaissance scientists stressed the absoluteness of natural laws.

Surprisingly, even the sixteenth-century Reformers contributed to the rise of humanism. Their success in stripping away Roman Catholic dogma and reviving apostolic theology, with its commitment to personal growth and renewal rather than to the "church," paved the way for questioning all religion and "won elbow room for both skeptics and secularists" by giving birth to the idea of toleration.[14]

Let me add that at this point in history, Renaissance philosophers and scientists were not seeking to overthrow Christianity. Peter Gay, in his classic book on the Enlightenment, stated:

> With few exceptions the Humanists remain within the Christian fold; the affection for pagan works did not make them pagans. . . . The central intellectual problem of the Renaissance was to find . . . a compromise formula . . . that would enable man to live comfortably with classical forms and Christian convictions, trust in man and trust in God, vigorous secular energies and a tenacious ascetic ideal.[15]

Gay went on to say:

> Classicism seems to have caused no religious turmoil
> within them. The sacred remained a central theme for Re-
> naissance sculptors, architects, and painters. . . . Donatello,
> Leonardo, Raphael, Michelangelo—the greatest of them,
> who had all absorbed the lessons of antiquity and the teach-
> ings of nature, lavished their genius on Madonnas, on
> Davids, on scenes from the Passion of Christ.[16]

By the time of the late Renaissance, although many churchmen could
not be considered totally orthodox, they nevertheless were still some distance from the Enlightenment view of Christianity. Gay commented further:

> While [seventeenth-century] Christianity was no longer
> quite the Christianity of the [earlier] Renaissance, its world-
> liness was not yet the secularism of the Enlightenment. . . .
> Even the revolutionary discoveries of seventeenth-century
> scientists were not in general regarded as subversive: many
> warm supporters of the "new learning" greeted the writing
> of Galileo, and later those of Newton, as evidence for the
> faith rather than a threat to it.[17]

The Enlightenment

The Renaissance and the Reformation planted the seeds that later
sprouted and matured into well-developed secular humanism during the
eighteenth-century Enlightenment.[18] Spearheaded by a loose, informal
group of religious skeptics, political reformers, and philosophers, such as
Voltaire (1694–1778), David Hume (1711–1776), Denis Diderot (1713–1784),
and Immanuel Kant (1724–1804), Enlightenment thinkers rejected the
authority of the Christian church and opened the door for the acceptance
of humanism.

The eighteenth-century philosophers differed among themselves, but
they had one thing in common: all of them rejected religion in general and
Christianity in particular. Their attacks against Christianity were relentless
and unmerciful. To eighteenth-century philosophers, "faith in the power of
reason to improve the lot of mankind was religion; whatever hindered the
spread of enlightenment was an obstacle to be destroyed, an idol to be
shattered."[19] Enlightenment scholar Ernest Cassirer noted: "If we were to
look for a general characteristic of the age of enlightenment, the traditional answer would be that its fundamental feature is obviously a critical
and skeptical attitude toward religions."[20]

In short, the Enlightenment witnessed a turning away from Christian orthodoxy. It broke the back of the Christian worldview prevalent in Western culture, especially among the philosophers, intellectuals, educators, scholars, and even many theologians. Scholar James Livingston summed it up well:

> The Enlightenment represents the loosening of the state and society from ecclesiastical control and the emergence of a culture largely secular in character. The theories and sanctions of modern social and political life are no longer derived from biblical revelation or Church authority but independently arrived at by natural reason and social experience. An essential feature of the Enlightenment and of our modern culture since the eighteenth century is the growing separation of Western civilization from the authority of Church and theological dogma.[21]

The Rise of Scientism

The only ingredient left to finish the recipe of fully developed secular humanism was some bonafide source of knowledge. (As we've seen, a source of truth is one of the six necessary ingredients of a worldview.) The philosophical assumptions were thoroughly articulated during the Enlightenment, but objective verification was needed to give secular humanism respectability. This last ingredient was added in the nineteenth century with the rise and acceptance of scientism.

Prior to Darwin's *The Origin of Species* (1859), science was considered among theologians as a handmaid rather than as an enemy of Christianity.[22] Dr. Langdon Gilkey of the University of Chicago Divinity School pointed out: "Most intelligent men, and so most 18th century scientists [as well as theologians], held that divine revelation could tell us what had happened in the beginning, how the Creator had, so to speak, set the stage of the world which their science was now newly investigating."[23]

However, after Darwin, all that changed. The theory of evolution offered an appealing and rational alternate explanation for the origin of life and the cosmos—including man. It introduced objective "proof" that the eighteenth-century philosophers were correct in their assessment that human beings were not the product of God. Human beings were the product of nature, and as such, they were masters of themselves.

The hypothesis that humans gradually developed from primitive life forms into highly intelligent and capable animals denied biblical teachings on Creation and the Fall. If we are not created, there is no God. If we are not fallen sinners, we have no need of a Savior. Quite the contrary, evolution shows that humanity is steadily improving. The future is bright. With a little more work and a little more knowledge, heaven and earth will become synonymous. We hold the key to a dazzling future, not God, and science is the tool to achieve it.

Let me sum this up. Evolution denies creation. A denial of creation is a denial of God. A denial of God elevates humanity to the status of supreme beings. People, not God, are sovereign, autonomous, and authoritative. People, not God, are the measure of all things. The result? The birth of a new religion grounded in naturalism: atheistic secular humanism.

The Consummation

It was not until the middle of the twentieth century that the combined forces of eighteenth-century philosophy and nineteenth-century scientism reached their full flowering. Secular humanism has enjoyed its most rapid growth, greatest influence, and widest acceptance in just the last fifty years.

The full *moral* impact of secular humanism, then, was not felt until after World War II. In fact, the radical and widely accepted ethical changes prevalent in Western culture today—changes away from traditional Christian ethics—did not greatly affect the average person until the 1960s. Society's move from the Christian worldview to secularism has been a slow jog over the past two centuries, suddenly bursting into a sprint in the last thirty years.

After fifteen centuries of dominance, Christianity is no longer the guiding force in Western culture. Secular humanism is now the dominant worldview. It's the filter through which modern people judge reality and the frame of reference by which they make decisions in all areas of life. Accordingly, here in the West, secular humanism defines social norms and practices and determines truth in ethical, religious, and other areas.

This is true even for people who claim to be theists, that is, for people who believe in God. In spite of their beliefs, most westerners, including many Christians, live lives more in sync with secular humanism than with theism.

The sad fact is, humanist assumptions have infiltrated many churches. During the late nineteenth and early twentieth centuries, many theologians attempted to accommodate Christian theology with naturalistic philosophy and evolution. Liberal theology crept into the church. Today, liberalism is well-entrenched in most mainline denominations. In these churches, the deity of Jesus Christ, the inerrancy and authority of Scripture, humanity's sin nature, the virgin birth, and a host of other cardinal beliefs are openly questioned and in some cases thrown out because they do not pass through secular humanism's worldview filter.

More than any other religion or philosophy, including the New Age Movement, secular humanism is Christianity's chief adversary. The question remains, however, does secular humanism correspond to reality? In spite of its dominant position in Western society, is it truth?

Doctrines of a "State" Religion

Like other religions, secular humanism is a belief accepted by faith. And like other religions, it possesses sacred writings: the *Humanist Manifesto I* (published in 1933) and the *Humanist Manifesto II* (published in 1973). They were written, to use their own words:

> In order that religious humanism . . . be better understood.
> . . . Today man's larger understanding of the universe, his scientific achievements, and his deeper appreciation of brotherhood, have created a situation which required a new statement of the means and purposes of religion. . . . To establish such a religion is a major necessity of the present. It is a responsibility which rests upon this generation. *(Humanist Manifesto I)*

Both *Manifestos* were signed by many of the leading educators, scientists, and philosophers of this century. Dr. Benjamin Spock, educator John Dewey, philosopher Antony Flew, prominent scientist Francis Crick, psychologist B. F. Skinner, ethicist Joseph Fletcher, and many others working in strategically powerful areas in public view. Because of their prominence, these pacesetters were able to influence public opinion far beyond their numerical strength.

Here's what the *Humanist Manifesto I and II* affirm about the six key features of a worldview that we have been examining. I will quote passages directly from *Humanist Manifesto I and II*.

God

"As in 1933, humanists still believe that traditional theism, especially faith in the prayer-hearing God, assumed to love and care for persons, to hear and understand their prayers, and to be able to do something about them, is an unproved and outmoded faith" *(Humanist Manifesto II)*.

"We find insufficient evidence for belief in the existence of a supernatural" *(Humanist Manifesto II)*.

Humanity

"Humanism believes that man is a part of nature and that he has emerged as the result of a continuous process" *(Humanist Manifesto I)*.

"As nontheists, we begin with humans not God, nature not deity" *(Humanist Manifesto II)*.

"Modern science discredits such historic concepts as the 'ghost in the machine' and the 'separable soul.' Rather, science affirms that the human species is an emergence from natural evolutionary forces" *(Humanist Manifesto II)*.

"The preciousness and dignity of the individual person is a central humanist value." "We are responsible for what we are or will be. . . . At the present juncture of history, commitment to all humankind is the highest commitment of which we are capable; it transcends the narrow allegiances of church, state, party, class, or race in moving toward a wider vision of human potential" *(Humanist Manifesto II)*.

In sum, we are self-sufficient. We don't need God; we can do it on our own.

Creation

"The universe is self-existing and not created" *(Humanist Manifesto I)*.

Evolution, which flows directly from naturalistic philosophy, permits humanists to explain our origins without God. It removes the desire or need to seek a theistic explanation for the origin of the universe or ourselves. It follows from this that if human beings have no creator they are indeed the "measure of all things." They are fully autonomous (self-governing and free to determine their own destiny), independent (not dependent on God), the creators of social and moral behavior (ethics are relative), and without accountability to God for their actions.

Suffering and Evil

Secular humanists reject the Christian understanding of sin, its origin, its historical significance, and its role in human actions. Because of their atheistic presuppositions, humanists reject any moral absolute by which ethical guidelines are universal in application.

"We are responsible for what we are or will be" *(Humanist Manifesto II)*.

"We affirm that moral values derive their source from human experience. Ethics is *autonomous* and *situational*, needing no theological or ideological sanction. Ethics stem from human need and interest" (i.e., ethics are relative; *Humanist Manifesto II*).

"In the area of sexuality, we believe that intolerant attitudes, often cultivated by orthodox religious and puritanical cultures, unduly repress sexual conduct. The right to birth control, abortion, and divorce should be recognized. . . . The many varieties of sexual exploration should not in themselves be considered 'evil.'. . . Short of harming others or compelling them to do likewise, individuals should be permitted to express their sexual proclivities and pursue their lifestyles as they desire" *(Humanist Manifesto II)*.

Thus, prostitution, homosexuality, and pornography are acceptable if one wishes to engage in them. Humanists also recognize "an individual's right to die with dignity, euthanasia, and the right to suicide" *(Humanist Manifesto II)*.

Salvation and Eternal Life

"Religious humanism considers the complete realization of human personality to be the end of man's life" *(Humanist Manifesto I)*.

"Promises of immortal salvation or fear of eternal damnation are both illusory and harmful. They distract humans from present concerns, from self-actualization, and from rectifying social injustices. . . . There is no credible evidence that life survives the death of the body. We continue to exist in our progeny and in the way that our lives have influenced others in our culture" *(Humanist Manifesto II)*.

Source of Truth

"The way to determine the existence and value of any and all realities is by means of intelligent inquiry and by the assessment of their relation to human needs [thus truth, like ethics, is relative]. Religion must formulate its shapes and plans in light of the scientific spirit and method [scientism]" *(Humanist Manifesto I)*.

"Any account of nature should pass the tests of scientific evidence; in our judgment, the dogmas and myths of traditional religions do not do so" *(Humanist Manifesto II)*.

"*Reason and intelligence* are the most effective instruments that humankind possesses. There is no substitute: neither faith nor passion suffices in itself. The controlled use of scientific methods, which have transformed the natural and social sciences since the Renaissance, must be extended further in the solution of human problems" *(Humanist Manifesto II)*.

Is There a Problem Here?

What's wrong with all this? Many things, but we only need to examine three problems with secular humanism to prove that it is not a viable worldview. In spite of the powerful and influential names endorsing the *Humanist Manifesto I and II,* and in spite of its "scientific" orientation, secular humanism does not explain many things which most people see as elements of reality.

First, secular humanism is both internally and externally inconsistent. Many of its truth-claims do not correspond to objective reality. Second, secular humanism fails to answer crucial questions about God and humanity in a way that is in harmony with reality as universally understood and lived out. Third, it is not subjectively satisfying—that is, it is does not meet people's spiritual needs. We will look at each of these briefly. Together, they will demonstrate that secular humanism is unable to sustain its truth-claims. As a worldview, it is not a contender for religious truth. It fails the worldview truth tests at which we have been looking.

Secular Humanism Is Inconsistent with Supernatural Reality

The most obvious way in which secular humanism is inconsistent with reality is its view of the supernatural. Humanists deny the existence of God and reject all things supernatural. Of course, this is a philosophical assumption that can't be proven.

So the question needs to be rephrased: Is there compelling evidence *for* the existence of God? If there is, can that evidence be tested? If so, and if atheists are unable to *disprove the evidence,* humanism's anti-supernatural presupposition crumbles.

Providing evidence for the existence of God is a foundational apologetic task that needs more space than what is available here. However, I have dealt with this subject elsewhere, and I encourage readers to investigate that material.[24] There is overwhelming empirical and philosophical evidence for God's existence. And if God exists, atheistic secular humanism can't reflect truth. The two positions are mutually exclusive, and for both to exist would violate the law of non-contradiction.

Humanism Fails to Answer Questions About God and Humanity

Humanism not only fails to refute the evidence confirming God's existence, but it also fails to answer other crucial questions about God and humanity. Here are two examples.

First, secular humanism not only fails to demonstrate that God doesn't exist, but it also fails to account for why people instinctively believe He does exist. This is a world-wide phenomenon. As we've seen, people everywhere and at all times have felt that God exists and have sought to understand Him and to have a relationship with Him.

Humanists claim that belief in God is either a psychological crutch stemming from people's inability to cope with life's disappointments, or it arises from primitive people's inability to understand physical phenomena and to explain the permanence of death. In either case, there is insufficient evidence to sustain these claims.

Belief in God is a natural response to an innate awareness of God that God Himself placed in the human psyche (Romans 1:19–20). C. S. Lewis and others have pointed out that every natural desire exhibited by human beings is a manifestation of a real and necessary human need. We crave spiritual fulfillment because God has placed this desire in us, just as we crave love and affection because it is in our nature to receive it. It is logical to assume that if we possess a natural desire for something in which the world offers no fulfillment, there is something outside the world that will fulfill it. We will have no longings that are unfulfillable, including spiritual longing.

The short of it is, secular humanism is out of touch with reality because it leaves a God-vacuum and because it can't account for God's persistence in the human psyche.

Second, secular humanism fails to account for our fallen nature, our *natural* tendency to sin. Why, after thousands of years of civilization, do people still interact negatively? Why don't we get along any better today than in the ancient past? If humanism reflects reality, this shouldn't be the case. Here's the reason why.

If human beings are the product of naturalistic evolution, then we should be improving—ethically, socially, and morally as well as physically. But if anything, we are worse off in these categories than ever before. Indeed, the torture and murder that occurred in the twentieth century alone under the *atheistic* political systems of Nazi Germany and Soviet Marxism is many millions more than throughout all the centuries of the Christian church combined. As Dr. Robert Morey stated, "Over one hundred and fifty million people in the last forty years have been killed by atheistic governments." [25]

Even the *Humanist Manifesto II,* written in 1973, concedes this:

> Events since then *[Humanist Manifesto I]* make earlier statements seem far to optimistic. Nazism has shown the depths of brutality of which humanity is capable. Other totalitarian regimes have suppressed human rights without ending poverty. Science has sometimes brought evil as well as good. Recent decades have shown that inhuman wars can be made in the name of peace. The beginning of police states, even in democratic societies, widespread government espionage, and other abuses of power by military, political, and industrial elites, and the continuance of unyielding racism, all present a different and difficult social outlook.

In learning to apply the scientific method to nature and human life, we have opened the door to ecological damage, overpopulation, dehumanizing institutions, totalitarian repression, and nuclear and biochemical disaster.

It's now been twenty-five years since the *Humanist Manifesto II* was written. The humanists' goal to use "technology wisely" in order to "control our environment, conquer poverty, markedly reduce disease, extend our life span, significantly modify our behavior, alter the course of human evolution and cultural development, unlock vast new powers, and provide humankind with unparalleled opportunity for achieving an abundant and meaningful life" is no closer today than it was in 1973 or 1933—or 1933 B.C., for that matter.

Sir Fred Catherwood, a member of the European Parliament for Cambridge and North Bedfordshire, made a timely comment:

> What we do know is that after a full generation the social experiments of the secular humanists are ripping society apart. They cannot produce a stable replacement moral order, and society cannot afford to allow the experiment to run any longer. If Christianity is only one point of view, then so is secular humanism. . . . The humanists have no agreed moral order and no organization through which they can deliver broad assent among a majority, and their track record of application to the social order is both brief and destructive.[26]

Humanism Is Not Spiritually Satisfying

A third way in which secular humanism fails the worldview test is that it is not spiritually satisfying. To fill the God-void created by secular humanism, people are reaching beyond the humanist worldview to embrace the religious teachings of other worldviews. This creates a problem for humanists. A consistent worldview must be spiritually satisfying. Otherwise, it's not corresponding to reality (in this case, the real human need for spiritual fulfillment).

When we examined the New Age Movement, we saw that it is essentially a religious movement in which people are attempting to synthesize their innate belief in God with their desire for human autonomy.

Philosophically, New Age followers accept most, if not all, of the propositions of secular humanists—except their rejection of God. They agree with humanists that we are the master of our own destiny, the universe is eternal, sin is the absence of right information, there are no moral absolutes (ethics are relative), there is no afterlife in the sense of physical existence, and truth flows from human judgments and experiences.

In light of our understanding of secular humanism, it is now clear that the New Age Movement entails a rebellion against *God-sterile* secular humanism. The New Age is not a rebellion against humanism itself, but rather against the God-vacuum created by secular humanism.

Secular humanism is not spiritually satisfying because it removes God. But if secular humanism fails in one of the most essential components of a worldview—the need to satisfy people's spiritual hunger—it must not reflect reality as it really exists. Humanism is not a viable worldview if it is not spiritually satisfying.

Why Can't Humanists and Christians Get Along?

Christians do not condemn the *goals* of humanists so long as they are in harmony with God's Word. Christians agree with humanists that "discrimination based upon race, religion, sex, age, or national origin" should be eliminated. We also "believe in the *right to universal education*" and that "everyone has a right to cultural opportunity to fulfill his or her unique capacities and talents." We also "deplore racial, religious, ethnic, or class antagonisms" and are "critical of sexism or sexual chauvinism—male or female. We believe in equal rights for both women and men to fulfill their unique careers and potentialities as they see fit, free of individual discrimination" *(Humanist Manifesto II)*.

Many of humanism's goals Christians can accept. But we *can't* accept the philosophy of naturalism that powers secular humanism. We condemn naturalism's unscientific, unrealistic, and anti-supernatural assumptions that reject God as well as attempts to foist this view on society. We reject humanism's notion that "at the present juncture of history, commitment to all humankind is the highest commitment of which we are capable; it transcends the narrow allegiances of church, state, party, class, or race in moving toward a wider vision of human potentiality" *(Humanist Manifesto II)*.

Secular humanism is a clear case of the means not justifying the ends. Rather the alleviating the woes of humanity, secular humanism has facilitated them. Sacrificing God at the altar of human ambition and self-exaltation is not only wrong, it doesn't work. Substituting ethical relativity for the moral absolutes of Scripture has resulted in millions of murdered unborn babies, the moral decadence of pornography and homosexuality, and the rapid depreciation and deterioration of the American family—the latter being the very backbone of Western society. Catherwood drove this point home:

> Humanism will fail because it is, like Marxism, an intellectual creed that does not correspond to the experience of ordinary people and does not give any answers that satisfy them to the great questions of good and evil, health and sickness, life and death. It can dissolve the bonds that hold society together, but it cannot put them together again. It tells people outraged by crime that it is a psychological

sickness that can be healed. It tells those who have no hope in this life that there is no hope after it; it tells those who live in dread of death that there is no life beyond death. It tells those who see design in nature that there is no designer, that, contrary to all human experience, order arose out of chaos. Above all, it teaches men and women, who were born to worship, that there is no God. So it cleans the house of the old, long-accepted religion, but leaves it open for the first new religion that comes along to enter and take possession (cf. Matt. 12:43–45).[27]

Over the past thirty years, as secular humanism moved dramatically onto center stage while Christianity shuffled meekly off into the wings, we have witnessed an unparalleled rise in sexual promiscuity—with resultant diseases and teenage pregnancies and suicides—divorce, all manners of crime, and burgeoning numbers of welfare recipients.[28] David Wells noted:

> The American way of life may be the envy of the world, its gadgets and accoutrements sought after and emulated, but the American version of happiness, it turns out, it quite lethal. America is a violent and disturbed country. Its teenagers have the highest suicide rate in the world (in 1991, more teenage boys died from gunshot wounds than from all natural causes combined); it leads the world in the consumption of drugs, legal and illegal, in addictions of various kinds, in divorce, in the incidence of depressive illness, and in the marketing of a vast range of therapies to counteract these problems. . . . [29]

Traditional American families have become endangered, and our legal system is a mockery of the original intent of our country's founding fathers, who, incidentally, took it for granted that God was the source of all law.[30]

Anyone who says that the world is better off practicing humanists' values and living humanists' lifestyles is either grossly naive, or they must stay indoors all day, everyday, and never read a newspaper, watch TV, or listen to the radio.

What Can We Do?

The expressed goal of secular humanism is the destruction of Christianity. In achieving this goal, it has infiltrated and influenced every area of

American life. Who would have guessed forty years ago that Americans in the 1990s would be free to kill their unborn; would be prohibited from bringing their religious principles and values into public schools and government agencies; that their religious symbols, such as crosses and nativity scenes, would be banned from public places; that their children would be taught that homosexuality and sex outside of marriage are not only acceptable but encouraged; and that the theater would be dominated by movies that graphically portray violence, nudity, and blasphemy?

Secular humanism is leading the entire globe down the primrose path to moral anarchy. Yet people seem determined to plunge off the cliff of sensible conduct into the ocean of ethical insanity. We have become like mindless lemmings, like stupid rodents following a satanic Pied Piper.

If Christians don't resist, Christianity as a social influence will vanish from the American scene. Rather than the guiding light of Western society, it will become a dim candle struggling to stay lit in a hurricane of humanist values. It's easy to despair.

Today's world has become so immersed in secular humanism that it seems an impossible task to lead society back to its Christian roots. But Christians are not called to be successful; we are called to be faithful. Our job is to be a light before the secular world (Matt. 5:16); God's job is to convict and convince (John 16:8–11). Our job is to serve the Master; God's job is to move history forward to achieve His ultimate plan of redemption.

There have been many other times in human history when society seemed beyond repentance, yet God has worked great miracles. This should be encouraging for Christians today.

A good example of this is England in the early part of the eighteenth century. Historian Williston Walker wrote:

> The condition of the lower classes was one of spiritual destitution. Popular amusements were coarse, illiteracy widespread, law savage in its enforcement, jails sinks of disease and iniquity. Drunkenness was more prevalent than at any other period in English history.[31]

Historian Earle Cairns noted:

> In the first half of the [eighteenth] century the death rate went up as cheap gin killed many and sent others to the "asylum." Gambling was rampant. . . . Bull-, bear-, fox-, and cock-baiting were regular pastimes, and a series of executions by hanging on Tyburn Hill was a gala occasion

for the whole family. It was indeed a "sick century," suspicious of theology and lacking fervor. [32]

Into this maelstrom of depravity and gross immorality stepped John Wesley (1703–91) and a handful of other faithful evangelists, and "there came such a religious revival that in a few years the whole character of English society . . . changed, and there came a period of great spiritual life and activity in the church."[33]

The history of the Christian church is full of revivals. God is sovereign, and He can make dramatic and speedy changes when His people unite in prayer and move boldly into action under the power and leading of the Holy Spirit. Here are a few essentials as we put on the full armor of God to battle secular humanism.

First, pray for revival, locally and worldwide. Pray for a softening of the hardness of heart and rebellion of secular humanists. Pray for our government, leadership, and schools. In particular, pray for wisdom and for the specific needs of those in authority. Pray for your continued commitment to God, for your discipline and obedience to His teachings, and that you will be a light to the humanists about you.

Second, get involved. This is done through the power of our vote as well as through becoming active in civic affairs—local, state, and national. As Catherwood said, "It is the job of Christian leaders in society in both church and state to expose the rhetoric of humanism for the fraud on society that it is."[34] At the very least, all Christians should initiate contact with their governmental representatives through phone calls and letters whenever an issue of moral or religious significance is being confronted.

Third, rescind the humanist indoctrination your children receive in public schools and television by instructing them in biblical principles and truths.[35] Help them to see why contemporary morality and naturalism, especially atheistic evolution, leads to spiritual and social degradation. Equip them to stand firm and to resist the bright lights and flashy dress of secular humanism; teach them how to respond to the aggressive attacks of secular humanists (1 Peter 3:15). This teaching should be done both at home and in church. The idea is not isolation—that never works—but education. We are instructed by Jesus Himself to live in the world but not be a part of it (John 17:14–19). To live in the world is to contend for the faith (Jude 3).

Let me add one other thought. Although we are instructed in Scripture to obey the laws of the land and to be obedient to governmental authorities (Rom. 13:1–7; 1 Peter 2:13–14), nowhere does God command us to do anything that is contrary to His higher law (Acts 5:29). If human governments violate God's higher law, we are not only free to resist them, but we are obligated to so (Acts 4:18–20; 5:27–29).

Government is an institution created by God (Rom. 13:1b) to protect us and to punish evil doers (v. 4). When it sets itself up autonomous from God, when it begins to act as the source of truth and authority independent of and in opposition to God, it is no longer fulfilling the purpose for its creation. In this case, the state itself is in rebellion against God and must be stopped. When, for example, the state endorses and funds abortion, it is in direct violation of God's explicit laws against murder (Exod. 20:13). We are justified to resist and to change godless human laws and to bring them into conformity with God's higher law. Francis Schaeffer said it bluntly: *"If a law is wrong, you must disobey it."*[36]

I want to close with the words of Steve Hallman. They sum up the conclusions of this chapter:

> Law and government must be based on principles outlined in the Scriptures, the Word of God rather than the word of man. Man is accountable to his Creator. The laws he makes and governments he established are to be based on higher laws deriving from his Maker.
>
> Where has been the Christian voice as we have moved swiftly toward an almost totally secular humanistic system of law? Where was the Christian witness as humanists successfully argued a doctrine of separation of church and state which excluded Christians from meaningful participation in the state? Maybe we had accepted the role assigned to us by the secular humanists—one in which we sit as quiet, harmless, passive observers while society moves toward total hedonism. But what is at stake here is whether we will remain a country accepting the Judeo-Christian concept of right and wrong, or turn our backs on centuries of progress to embrace practical atheism. Our nation will reap what we sow.
>
> We can base our law and justice, our determination of right and wrong, on Holy Scripture—especially on the Ten Commandments and the Sermon on the Mount—or we can base our law and justice, our determination of right and wrong, on the humanist values of our day. But we cannot have both. They are diametrically opposed to each other.[37]

CHAPTER TWELVE

Postmodernism: God Is Whoever

My apologetics library is not large, just under two hundred books, but it is current and varied. Out of curiosity I recently scanned these books to see how many authors referred to postmodernism. I also looked in the subject index and the table of contents of every book that I thought might mention one or more of three related concepts: postmodernism, relativism, and pluralism. What I found was not surprising.

Only twenty-two books listed at least one of these topics (relativism being the most common by a wide margin). Of these, eleven were published in the 1990s, nine in the 1980s, and two in the 1970s. Only five of the books actually included the term *postmodernism* in their indexes, and all of those were written in the 1990s.

A few years ago, postmodernism as a distinct apologetic issue was not included in any apologetic book. It wasn't even included in the first draft of *this* book. But I've come to realize that it is probably the most important and timely topic that I am covering.

Why do I feel this way? Because postmodernism is the newest, most aggressive, and most urgent issue facing the church in modern times. Every Christian has come in contact with—and has been adversely affected by—this belief system.

It's not just the church that is in jeopardy. This flourishing and persuasive belief system is launching a worldview shift of such magnitude that it is literally changing the fundamental presuppositions that have governed

Western thought for three centuries. It is influencing every area of knowledge: science, education, sociology, psychology, history, law, and even entertainment and the media.

In order to set the stage for this topic, we must return briefly to secular humanism.

Secular Humanism

We saw in the previous chapter that from the fourth to the eighteenth century, Christianity was the dominant worldview in Western culture. Beginning during the Enlightenment, however, secular humanism began to exert increasing influence. Today, it has emerged as the dominant worldview in the West.

We also saw that one of the defining attributes of secular humanism is that it rests on the philosophical foundation of naturalism. Among other things, secular humanism adheres to the philosophy that human reasoning alone can discover absolute truth—everything there is to know about science, morality, and human behavior. This view is often referred to as *modernism*.

In terms of religion, modernism teaches that "religious beliefs are rational if and only if one has evidence on which those beliefs are based."[1] However, since most secular humanists believe that there is no valid evidence for the existence of God, religious belief is effectively defined out of existence. Hence, secular humanism is essentially a godless worldview.

In the past, when Christians challenged this assumption, they fought it out with secularists on a level playing field. Both sides mustered evidence to support their particular view. They applied the laws of logic, employed human reasoning, and debated the issue in books, articles, lectures, seminars, college classrooms, and other public formats.

Although Christians and secularists disagreed on what is truth, both agreed that ultimate truth existed in every area of knowledge and that it could be discovered and understood. They also agreed that truth was absolute and objective—it existed independent of people's personal beliefs or experiences. To secular humanists, truth was learned through human reasoning. To Christians, ultimate truth was a product of divine revelation. But both Christians and secularists agreed that truth was rational, accessible, and adhered to fundamental laws of logic. Neither objected to evidence or reasoning.

Postmodernism

In recent years a new worldview has emerged that is aggressively challenging and forcefully changing traditional secular humanism. It is a movement away from modernism because it rejects human reasoning as an invincible avenue to truth. This new approach to reality assumes that the human mind is *incapable* of apprehending truth in any absolute sense. Why is this? According to this view, there is no absolute truth to apprehend! And even if there was, it could not be known. Thus truth is subjective rather than objective, inaccessible by human reasoning rather than accessible.

This evolving worldview is referred to as *postmodernism* because it has emerged out of and moves beyond modernism. It is an entirely different way of viewing reality, and it is an increasingly major obstacle to Christian evangelism. Indeed, it is becoming a serious issue *within* the church. Thousands of Christians are unwittingly assimilating postmodern philosophy into their thinking, causing them to compromise ethical behavior (moral relativism), reject the uniqueness of Christianity (religious pluralism), and dismiss the Bible in favor of religious experiences (religious subjectivism).

The Danger of Postmodernism

Many Christian apologists fear that this growing movement is fast becoming the most dangerous adversary Christianity has ever faced, primarily because postmodernism endorses religious pluralism. It teaches that all religious truth-claims are equally legitimate—even when they blatantly contradiction one another. Moreover, postmodernists fiercely condemn anyone who challenges this assumption. The door to religious analysis and appraisal is tightly locked. It is simply politically incorrect for one religion to claim ultimate truth at the exclusion of all others.

I want to begin this discussion of postmodernism with a lengthy quote from Dennis McCallum's recent book *The Death of Truth.*[2] It sets the stage by describing what could happen if the present generation of Christian apologists do not respond to this aggressive and dangerous attack:

> Within the months after Charles Darwin released his *Origin of the Species* in 1859, a revolution in thinking gripped the scientific world. Although at the time most Christians had no idea anything was happening, no one today doubts the far-reaching results of that revolution. During the decades after Darwin, the notion of a natural world with no place for God became a new, nearly unanimous understanding among intellectuals, eventually reshaping every academic discipline, as well as education, government, and even the church. Now, by the close of the twentieth century, even popular culture accepts Darwin's theory of naturalistic evolution as settled fact.

The Christian church wasn't ready for Darwin. . . . Early Christian apologists in this field often showed a lack of understanding of what natural selection was, not to mention the reasons people believed in it. Christians couldn't respond in a convincing way to a doctrine they understood only dimly, and when we look back at some of the arguments Christians first advanced against the doctrine of naturalistic evolution, we can only grimace in embarrassment.

Most Christians today can answer evolutionists effectively, but their ability to change minds on this issue is minimal. Why? Too much time passed without a coherent, credible Christian voice to counteract Darwin's theory. Darwinism managed to distance God from creation and the natural world—with the effect that even people who hold a dim belief that God exists regard him as irrelevant to their daily lives. We can only wonder what would have happened if some of the current sophisticated, convincing Christian arguments were at hand when Darwin first wrote.

Unfortunately, Christian leadership wasn't ready for the intellectual challenges of the late nineteenth century, with devastating results.

Now, in the late twentieth century, we are caught up in a revolution that will likely dwarf Darwinism in its impact on every aspect of thought and culture: *postmodernism.* Unlike Darwinism, postmodernism isn't a distinct set of doctrines or truth claims. It is a *mood*—a view of the world characterized by a deep distrust of reason, not to mention a disdain for knowledge Christians believe the Bible proves. . . .

Just as Darwinism wasn't easy to understand 150 years ago, postmodernism and its impact isn't immediately easy to grasp.[3]

So what precipitated this revolutionary move away from the modernist view that truth is objective and attainable through reason to the postmodernist view that truth is subjective and inaccessible through reason? Theologian Alister McGrath explained the change with these words:

The rise of the movement which is now generally known as "postmodernism" throughout the Western world is a direct result of the collapse of this confidence in reason, and a more general disillusionment with the so-called "modern" world. Postmodernism is the intellectual movement which proclaims, in the first place, that the Enlightenment rested on fraudulent intellectual foundations (such as the belief in the omni-competence of human reason), and in the second, that it ushered in some of the most horrific events in human history—such as the Stalinist purges and the Nazi extermination camps.[4]

Today, postmodernism is well-entrenched. Yet it is a relatively new philosophy—at least in terms of influencing culture. There is time to formulate and initiate an apologetics to postmodernism. We dare not wait, lest postmodern philosophy becomes as ingrained in our thinking as Darwinism.

In the following pages we will give a basic introduction to this significant worldview and offer a few suggestions on how Christian apologists may formulate a defense. I hope the discussion will also stimulate further research into this rapidly expanding and highly contagious worldview.[5]

What Postmodernists Believe

Postmodernism promotes an entirely different worldview with entirely different presuppositions than traditional, naturalistic secular humanism (modernism). Modernists see reality as possessing universal and absolute truths. Human reasoning is the key to apprehending these truths, and it depends on the laws of logic. Hence, logical inferences are valid, legitimate, and trustworthy; truth is objective and attainable.

Postmodernists, on the other hand, see truth as wholly pluralistic and relativistic. They reject the concept of a universe where reality can be apprehended entirely through rational processes—human reasoning. There is no universal or absolute truth in any area of knowledge, including science, history, psychology, sociology, ethics, and religion.

Postmodernists believe that truth has its source in human ideas and experiences, as interpreted through individual cultures, rather than in a source outside human thoughts and feelings—such as God. They assume that contradicting beliefs can be true at the same time—as they must, if truth depends on people, and people have different opinions on what is truth.

The following chart may help you see the difference between postmodernism and modernism.

Postmodernism vs. Modernism

Forms:	Modernism	Postmodernism
Beliefs:	Objective	Subjective
	Reasoning	Non-reasoning
	Truth universal	Truth non-universal
	People primarily physical beings	People primarily social beings
Foundational Presuppositions:	Naturalism	Pluralism and Relativism

Why Postmodernists Believe As They Do

Postmodernists believe that people are so dynamically bound to their culture and to their social structures that reality and culture are inseparable. People are a product of what their culture makes them; cultures determine—create—people's thoughts and attitudes. Thus, people think only in terms of what they assimilate and interpret through their culture.

For example, Americans see themselves as individualistic and self-sufficient. This is likely the result of the American frontier experience, where centuries of westward movement encouraged the development of independent thinking, cultural mobility, and the myth that all people have an equal opportunity to be successful if they don't give up.

The reason postmodernists believe there is no objective or absolute or universal truth is because they see all truth as relative and a product of cultural beliefs. People are totally incapable of separating what they think is objectively true from their cultural bias. Thus, wrote McGrath, "All interpretations are . . . equally valid, or equally meaningless (depending upon your point of view)."[6]

To a postmodernist, truth is wholly *subjective*. It flows from personal opinions and experiences as it passes through and is interpreted by one's cultural worldview. Since all cultures differ, there is no single truth applicable to everyone. As apologist Jim Leffel put it, "Truth isn't discovered, but manufactured."[7]

The result is that we cannot judge other cultures in terms of their social, religious, and ethical behavior because our reality is simply different from theirs. All systems of belief are equally true.

The Role of Language

One of the key presuppositions of postmodernism is that truth is tightly bound to language. Because language varies from culture to culture, so does truth. Let me explain.

Postmodernists point out that people communicate and think through language. Different cultures have words with entirely different meanings. Some culture have specific words with specific meanings that are completely absent in other cultures. For example, Eskimos may have a dozen words for ice, each with a different meaning depending on conditions. This is a result of cultural needs—living with ice and communicating icy conditions is essential for Eskimo survival.

Because people think in words, and these words vary from culture to culture, people see reality differently. This further precludes the existence of universal truths that are applicable to all cultures. In other words, "Different language systems lead to different ways of thinking [so] we lose the ability to judge the ideas of other cultures. To do so would be to impose our own language and thought patterns on their way of thinking."[8]

A Hidden Agenda

In spite of this relativistic and pluralistic view of human autonomy, postmodernists have a political agenda. They, too, want to effect change on society.

Most postmodernists see Western culture as repressive to minorities and other socially restricted groups. They claim that Western culture (American and European) dominates the world scene and thus exerts its power (its truths) over oppressed cultures (including subcultures within the larger Western culture—such as minorities, women, and homosexuals). The result is that Western culture promotes its privileged position in world society at the expense of the oppressed. This needs to be changed, postmodernists claim, so that all people are truly equal in terms of opportunities and freedom.

Although a worthy goal in and of itself, and one with which most Christians would agree, nevertheless many postmodernists' goals—and certainly the methods for achieving them—are diametrically opposed to Christian principles and truths.

A good example of this is the well-known (but misunderstood) concept of politically correct speech. Contrary to what many people think, the goal of politically correct speech is *not* to teach sensitivity to people's feelings. Rather, its purpose is to change society. "The Political-correctness movement isn't just an attempt to keep from hurting people's feelings, but an attempt to create different kinds of people by changing the cultural environment."[9]

According to postmodernists, since people communicate ideas through language, if you want to change society you change the way people talk. This in turn will change the way they think and behave: "Language is not neutral but a tool by which those in power or in control of the media can manipulate and construct reality."[10] To put it another way, words don't allow us to apprehend truth—they change truth. Changing languages actually creates new reality: "In the end, language cannot authoritatively communicate reality 'as it is'; rather, it fabricates what 'really is.'"[11]

The danger of the so-called politically correct movement is the sacrifice of truth in order to preserve a social-political agenda. McGrath pointed out:

> To allow criteria such as "tolerance" and "openness" to be given greater weight than "truth" is, quite simply, a mark of intellectual shallowness and moral irresponsibility. The first, and most fundamental, of all questions must be: is it true? Is this worthy of belief and trust? Truth is certainly no guarantee of relevance—but no one can build his or her personal life around a lie. A belief system, however consoling and reassuring, may prove to be false in itself, or rest upon utterly spurious foundations. . . . It will be a sad day when a claim to be telling the truth is met with the reply that there is no truth to tell, or that telling the truth is tantamount to oppression."[12]

You see, some truth simply cannot be allow to pass unchallenged. If it flies in the face of universal human experience, reason, and judgment, and of what people normally recognize and condemn as unacceptable behavior, it's not truth at all. McGrath continued:

> There must be some criteria, some standards of judgment, which allow one to exclude certain viewpoints as unacceptable. Otherwise, postmodernism will be seen to be uncritical and naive, a breeding ground of the political and moral complacency which allowed the rise of the Third Reich back in the 1930s.[13]

Postmodernism in the Future

Postmodernism is widely accepted by the pacesetters in our colleges and universities. Academicians in growing numbers are rejecting modernism and embracing postmodernism. These are the people whose thoughts and ideas eventually trickle down to the average person on the street, shaping and reshaping worldviews on religion, law, politics, morality, education, and practically everything else.

As Leffel noted, "Lest we think that postmodernists are academics or activists 'out there' somewhere, we need to note that today we are fast becoming a *postmodern culture*. Our culture widely accepts the basic tenants of postmodernism."[14]

Unless Christians formulate a compelling and aggressive apologetics to postmodernism, we will see major social changes far more influential and dangerous in terms of their impact on Christianity than the results of the Darwinian revolution in the nineteenth century have already been.

Summary of Postmodernism

Jim Leffel summarized the main tenants of postmodernism with these five points:

- Reality is in the mind of the beholder. Reality is what's real to me, and I construct my own reality in my mind.
- People are not able to think independently because they are defined—"scripted," molded—by their culture.
- We cannot judge things in another culture or in another person's life, because our reality may be different from theirs. There is no possibility of "transculture objectivity."
- We are moving in the direction of progress, but are arrogantly dominating nature and threatening our future.
- Nothing is ever proven, either by science, history, or any other discipline.[15]

So now that we understand the basics of postmodernism, how do we defend against it? Let me suggest some approaches that would work well in pointing out the flaws underlying the main tenants of postmodernism.

Reasoning Unreasonably

Leffel pointed out that "of all the questions raised by postmodern thought, the most fundamental is its critique of reason. . . . If postmodern skeptics are right, there can be no basis for knowledge of *any* kind. In postmodern culture, truth as we know it is dead."[16]

Postmodernists reject all objective truth: truth that exists independent of human thoughts or human experiences, and truth that is true whether one believes it or not. This foundational presupposition of postmodernism, then, is where our apologetics should begin. Must we totally reject human reasoning as an avenue to truth? No.

We saw in chapter five that human reasoning (rationalism) and human experience are not valid avenues to discovering *religious* truth. Christians believe that ultimate truth lies with God and is knowable primarily through divine revelation.

Nevertheless, Christians also recognize that human beings, by virtue of being created in the image of God, do possess the ability to think rationally. If we couldn't, we would be unable to either apprehend or to comprehend divine revelation. As Leffel pointed out, the achievements of modern science and technology—sophisticated computers, powerful machines, advances in medicine—all point to "an essentially reliable correspondence between our ideas of reality and reality itself."[17]

Human reasoning, although not an avenue to religious truth, is valid and reliable in the realm of science, technology, and other fields of inquiry. It is by our God-given ability to reason that we can investigate, experiment, and discover universal truths that are applicable to every culture.

Postmodernists' position on human reasoning is actually a self-defeating proposition. The only way they can deny the validity of reason is to employ reason. The postmodern claim that reason can't lead to absolute truth is an absolute statement about truth and reasoning! As McCallum pointed out, "Postmodern preachers declare that if we find anyone claiming to know truth, that person we should ignore. By their own test they should be ignored!"[18]

Inconsistencies Equal Untruths

One of the qualifying ingredients in any valid worldview is that people live consistently with its presuppositions. Their moral values and how they behave must be in harmony with what they believe—not contradict it. This raises yet another major flaw in postmodernism. Postmodernism promotes relativism and pluralism, but its disciples fail to live consistently with these philosophies. McGrath illustrated this:

> Even the most tolerant pluralist has difficulties with that aspect of Hinduism which justifies the inequalities of Indian society by its insistence upon a fixed social order, or forcibly burning alive a widow on her late husband's funeral pyre.[19]

Here's the problem, as William Watkins pointed out so clearly in his book *The New Absolutes*. Americans talk the talk of relativism, but walk the walk of absolutism. They expect *all* people to adhere to certain standards of behavior whether they want to or not. This is absolutism. People claim to be relativistic, but "what we see is the opposite of what we would rightly expect to find [if this were true]. The behavior of Americans betray their real commitments, and *relativism is not one of them*. We can see this in a variety of areas."[20]

Watkins offered this example: "After all, criminals are only living according to their code of conduct. What could be wrong with that? Nothing, if relativism is true. . . . In 1989 alone, 18 million lawsuits were filed in state and federal courts. . . . Does this sound like a people committed to the live-and-let-live attitude of relativism?"[21]

If our society were truly relativistic, our educational system would encourage people to examine all sides of an issue, such as evolution versus creation. But it doesn't. Teaching creation is forbidden in public schools. In a relativistic society, people would shun promoting their particular views on moral issues. Yet "homosexual advocates . . . write books, articles, editorials, and movie scripts to convince others of their viewpoint."[22] Likewise, in a relativistic world, countries would be free to deal with each other as they see fit. If this were true, "under the rule of relativism, the Nuremberg trials for Nazi war crimes could not have taken place. Neither would we be able to judge Croatians, Serbs, or Bosnians for acts of atrocity they committed against one another."[23]

In short, relativism, followed to its logical conclusion, inevitably leads to moral anarchy. No one wants that. Relativism and its bedfellow pluralism are philosophies that no sane person lives with consistently. When postmodernists are forced to bring their philosophical assumptions out of their ivory tower and live with them in the real world of blood, sweat, and tears, postmodernism is clearly seen as inconsistent and damaging.

Setting the Prisoners Free

A third erroneous assumption of postmodernism is its claim that people are prisoners of culture and language. Again, McCallum has provided the proper response:

> People are *influenced* by their culture, but examples abound of individuals who have turned against the views of their own culture, thus demonstrating a love of individual freedom.[24]

McCallum recognized that people make major worldview shifts all the time. Every religious conversion is a change in worldview. Historically, immigrants who come to America and become American citizens set aside their former cultural worldview to embrace American culture and language. Indeed, it is postmodern thinking—the separatist attitude of preserving one's cultural traditions in spite of their relevance—that encourages minorities and immigrants to adhere to their cultural roots at the expense of assimilating themselves into American culture.

Unethical Ethics

As in pluralism and relativism in general, postmodernism is unable to establish or to enforce ethical standards. To go a step further, if there are no moral absolutes—if all supposed "truths" are culturally relative—maintaining world-wide ethical standards is impossible. The Hitlers and Saddam Husseins of the world will have free reign.

But most of the world's people believe that moral standards are absolute and should apply to all nations. The alternative is moral anarchy. (Because the response to postmodernism in the area of ethics is the same as the response to moral relativism, refer to chapter three for a longer discussion of this topic.)

The Problem That Won't Go Away

The greatest challenge historically to Christianity is the problem of evil: How can an all-powerful, all-loving God tolerate evil and suffering? He must not be able to stop it, or if He can, He doesn't want to. In either case, it proves He doesn't exist as Christians believe.

This particular attack against Christianity is still the most frequently used by atheists to disprove the existence of God.[25] But it is precisely here, in the reality of suffering and evil, that postmodernism as a worldview fails most miserably.

Postmodernists reject universal moral absolutes—any ethical guidelines that transcend human beings and that are applicable to all people. In terms of the problem of evil, this means three things.

First, postmodernists are unable to identify what is evil. Postmodernism teaches that evil is relative to individuals or to circumstances. But circumstances and people's views of evil vary. Thus it's impossible to say that anything is actually evil. In other words, if there is no absolute standard of right and wrong (i.e., God), there is no criteria by which to determine what is evil.

Second, postmodernists are unable to issue judgments against evil. Again, if there is no moral absolute outside of human capriciousness and if evil can't be identified as evil, it's impossible judge, condemn, or punish evil. As Miethe and Habermas observed, "In the absence of ethical absolutes . . . the real presence of profound suffering is not actually something that is objectively *wrong*. So while pain would still be real (not an illusion) it is simply a reality devoid of any *ethical* consequences."[26]

Third, postmodernists cannot offer a solution to the problem of evil. In a postmodern world, evil and suffering are reduced to either products of evolution—a natural way to weed out physically and emotionally inferior people—or simply the "personal dissatisfaction of certain aspects of reality."[27] In either case, postmodernism offers no solution to the problem of evil. People are condemned to live out their lives in a universe where pain and suffering can surface unexpectedly and dramatically at any moment, and there is no hope of comfort or solution—now or in the future.

The Subjective Approach

Postmodernism has a built-in safeguard against truth-testing. If all cultural (or individual) truths are accepted a priori as equally valid, there is no way to prove that what one perceives to be true may in fact be false. For example, people who insist that Christianity and Hinduism are "different paths to the same mountaintop" (i.e., God) have rejected the law of non-contradiction, and no amount of rational argumentation will change their minds. Their thinking goes along these lines:

What's true for me is just as true as what's true for you. So we're both right. God is both monotheistic and pantheistic! I have no problem with that. If you do, it's because you're stuck in the rut of eighteenth-century rationalism and are unable to see that we create our own truths.

These individuals are unwilling to consider rational apologetic arguments. And for very good reason. Such arguments are meaningless in a pluralistic, relativistic world that denies absolute truths. In such cases our apologetic tactics will have to be *subjective* instead of objective. We must appeal to the heart since the mind is already made up.

Many apologists believe that evidence and rational argumentation are ineffective with postmodernists. As one author put it:

Christian apologetics in the modern world . . . assumed that a human being standing alone could be convinced by rational argumentation of the validity of Christian truth. It fit well with the Enlightenment assumptions about human beings and the priority of rationalism as a method of epistemology. While it may have worked . . . for that period of history, such an apologetic does not appear to be working for a world in which pure rationality is suspect and in which pluralism only exacerbates claims to truth.[28]

How do we apply a subjective approach to apologetics? By engaging "our contemporaries in their own social world by speaking to their plight of angst, despair, meaninglessness and spiritual hopelessness. . . . Christian apologetics must address the sociological as well as the intellectual realities of our contemporary culture."[29]

The subjective approach to apologetics attempts to convince unbelievers that Christianity offers solutions to the very issues postmodernism can't solve, such as the heart-wrenching problems of human suffering and evil. But rather than relying on evidence and argumentation, subjective apologists try to demonstrate the feasibility of Christianity through emotive avenues. Here are a few examples:

"Reading maketh a full man" (Francis Bacon). Christian apologists can encourage postmodernists to read Christian fiction that addresses particular social issues, such as Charles Colson's *Gideon's Torch.* Or they may suggest books that reveal Christian concepts and principles through fantasy and modern myths. C. S. Lewis's *The Chronicles of Narnia* and J. R. R. Tolkien's *The Lord of the Rings* are contemporary examples. True-life accounts, such as Corrie ten Boom's *The Hiding Place*, show the power of Christian faith and perseverance through God's grace.

Philosophical and moral speculation. Another subjective approach is to engage postmodernists in philosophical and moral speculation:

> *Why should anyone believe anything at all?*
> *What is the solution to the problem of evil if God doesn't exist?*
> *Is the degradation of women as promoted in some cultures equally true as Christianity's teaching on the equally of women?*
> *Is the Hindu lack of compassion for human life on the lower rungs of the social ladder as true as the Christian worldview that seeks to help the poor and downtrodden?*
> *Is perverse and harmful sexual behavior as true as God-created norms for sexual conduct?*

Lifestyle evangelism. Building relationships with unbelievers is a crucial part of any witnessing, but it can be especially meaningful to postmodernists. If our lives demonstrate that Christianity offers an inner peace and contentment that postmodernism fails to produce, Christianity can be extremely appealing to people who have never been responsive to apologetic evidence.

When we become involved in people's lives, when we reach out to share in people's suffering, when we come alongside in times of tragedy to comfort and encourage—when we simply do what Jesus instructs us to do— we create an environment that sets the Holy Spirit free to soften people's hearts and to open their minds to Christ.

Personal testimonies. Personal testimonies can make the objective side of our faith subjectively real. Telling postmodernists that Jesus can heal emotional wounds or deliver them from the bondage of drugs and alcohol may not illicit a response. They may not doubt such claims, but other religions say the same thing. Aren't they equally true? But when we share our personal experiences in these areas, truth becomes more than mere propositional statements. Christianity becomes emotionally and spiritually real.

The Spiritual Side of Postmodernism

Postmodernism is not a religious movement. Nevertheless, its disciples can actually be more open to the Christian message than modernists. Whereas secular humanism is atheistic by definition, postmodernism is not "stridently antispiritual or antisupernatural, as is evidenced by the growing popularity of New Age thinking."[30]

Postmodernists often have an openness to spiritual truth and are actively seeking spiritual fulfillment. This is why many postmodernists endorse New Age philosophy. In fact, the New Age Movement can be considered the spiritual side of postmodernism. Both rose out of the ashes of the Christian worldview. Both share essential doctrines: the divinity of humanity (people can create their own reality), moral relativity, and a subjective approach to truth. New Age religions make postmodernism spiritually palatable.

A Final Thought

Having acknowledged the value of subjective apologetics in the postmodern world, let me close with this. Certainly the subjective approach to apologetics is of great value—and it may become increasingly so if modern culture continues along its pluralistic, relativistic path.

Nevertheless, many so-called postmodernists are open to a rational, objective approach to truth. This is because they have not fully divorced themselves from modernism and still believe in the dependability of rational thought.

What has been said should not be construed to diminish or weaken the overall thrust of this book: The traditional, rational, evidential approach to apologetics is the key apologetic tactic in confronting contemporary people. The majority of people on the street still view the world through modernist eyes. Even people who openly endorse postmodernism and argue for relativism do not live consistently with this philosophy—especially when it conflicts with *their* self-interests.

Although religious pluralism and moral relativism are quickly becoming ingrained in modern culture, the majority of people still think in terms of absolutes and accept the reality of logic and reason. These people need their intellectual obstacles to faith removed.

CHAPTER THIRTEEN

"Death *May* Be Worse than Life"

The saying goes that there are two absolutes in life: death and taxes. I'm not so sure about the second one—some people have a talent for out-maneuvering the IRS—but there's no doubt about the first: No one gets out of *this* life alive. As philosopher William James put it, "Old age has the last word."[1]

In saying this, James wasn't just making a lighthearted comment on the inevitability of death. He wanted his readers to see that eventually we all face the fear, reality, and drama of ultimate death. He continued with these sobering words:

> The purely naturalistic look at life, however enthusiastically it may begin, is sure to end in sadness. . . . The old man, sick with an insidious internal disease, may laugh and quaff his wine at first as well as ever, but he knows his fate now, for the doctors have revealed it; and the knowledge knocks the satisfaction out of all these functions. They are partners of death and the worm is their brother, and they turn to a mere flatness.[2]

Some full-blooded atheists are so committed to naturalism that they deny any form of life after death. I suspect they are few and far between. Even those who cling to secular humanism as a worldview generally believe in some kind of deity and draw the line at absolute atheism. They call themselves agnostics, skeptics, or whatever, but in the deepest recesses of their hearts, they believe (or at least hope) that they will somehow outfox the Grim Reaper by moving into another dimension of conscious existence after death.

The late Edward John Carnell said it well:

> Something inside cries out against the conclusion that a purpose-seeking man has been hatched by a purposeless universe. The urge may be ill founded; it may have to be disqualified. Yet, there it is: Our heart tells us that there are destinies at stake in this life. We cannot eradicate this voice. Wisdom dictates, therefore, that before one decides whether or not this witness is trustworthy, a thorough investigation be conducted; lest through either oversight or default an everlasting loss in the soul be sustained.[3]

This innate yearning for the transcendent is exposed even in the lives of some of the most notorious atheists. Friedrich Nietzsche "found his atheism unbearable. Sartre, too, complained of the seeming unlivability of his position, declaring that 'atheism is a cruel and long-range affair.'"[4]

The traditional way to seek an answer to the question, "What happens to *me* after death?" has been through religion, particularly here in the West through the Christian religion. However, Western culture is now dominated by a secular worldview, and atheistic naturalism is the favored source of ultimate truth. Many people no longer accept Christianity as an avenue to truth and instead seek answers to life's great mysteries through science or nontraditional religions such as the cults and the New Age Movement.

But out of the myriad of religions and secular worldviews, only one can actually reflect truth. People who claim that they are being open-minded by accepting all religions as gateways to truth are actually being empty-headed. It's logically impossible for religious worldviews that contradict to both be right. And when we reject logic, it doesn't make everything true; it makes nothing true. God either exists or He doesn't exist. He is either the God of Christianity or some other God, but He can't be two different kinds of Gods at the same time. Logic, experience, and science don't operate in contradiction and neither can religion. If we are to make heads-or-tails out of reality and if religious truth is to be known at all, we must adhere to the rudimentary rules of logic that govern all other areas of knowledge.

We have demonstrated beyond reasonable doubt that only Christianity is internally and externally consistent, logical in its approach to reality, and in harmony with human experience as universally understood and lived out. Moreover, only the Christian worldview is confirmed by applying the scientific method to discovering truth; that is, only Christianity is verified to the highest level of certainty possible by historical, legal, scientific, and rational evidence.

In these last pages, I want to review a couple points and further emphasize the urgency of considering "the faith which was once for all delivered to the saints" (Jude 3).

Christianity Is Objectively True

Christianity is the only religion that is grounded on historical facts—facts that can be checked out. It alone among the world's religions can verify its truth-claims with concrete, objective, *nonbiblical* evidence. All other religions lack the precise and explicit historical, scientific, legal, rational, textual, archaeological, and prophetic testimonies that verify Christian truth-claims.

For example, how do we know Jesus Christ is God? Because He demonstrated it through His resurrection, and His resurrection is confirmed by historical evidence (Rom. 1:4). Jesus' birth, life, ministry, death, and post-resurrection appearances were observed by eyewitnesses and recorded in the Bible. Can we trust the Bible? We certainly can. By all the canons of acceptable historical investigation, its reliability and authenticity have been confirmed. No other religious document, ancient or modern, comes close to the Bible's verifiability.

But there are other ways to approach the objective reality of the Christian worldview. The Bible teaches that God created us for a purpose: to love us, to have a relationship with us, and for us to love, worship, and obey Him in return. God also presented us with a plan of salvation through Jesus Christ.

If all this is true and if God wants us to understand it, we can expect Him to reveal this information in a way that is easily understood by everyone. This means that revelation would be clear. It would not be esoteric or violate the laws of logic. We would not have to rely on priests or gurus or spirit guides to interpret it. Revelation would be complete and final. It would flow through prophets who didn't make mistakes—all their prophecies would come to pass exactly as described. This revelation would be recorded so that we would have an inerrant written record available to all generations of believers. This would allow it to be the absolute and authoritative standard from which all truth could be measured. This record would contain no inaccuracies or contradictions with regard to historical, scientific, geographical, cultural, or other information. In fact, we would expect these facts to be verified by evidence that could be tested.

I have just described Christian revelation.

Now, compare this with other religions. To begin with, many counterfeit revelations are esoteric and require a priest, guru, or prophet to interpret them. The ordinary believer is set apart from the priestly class. This should be expected if so-called revelation comes from humans rather than God. Non-Christian religions that tout prophecy, such as Mormonism and the Jehovah's Witnesses, have a long list of unfilled and inaccurate prophecies. Sacred writings in other religions are full of fanciful tales and historical and scientific inaccuracies. They are fraught with additions and deletions made as religious leaders sought to accommodate their teachings to changing values and goals. Finally all non-Christian religious books are unsupported by objective, verifiable evidence. They can't be checked out for truthfulness.

Which revelation—Christian or non-Christian—is objectively true? The answer is obvious.

The Christian worldview is also objectively true because it confirms reality as we understand it and live it out. Take, for example, the undeniable presence of sin and evil. Many Eastern religions and the New Age claim that people are innately divine, naturally good, and that evil and human suffering are illusions. Eventually, they say, good will prevail and heaven on earth will arrive.

The Bible, on the other hand, teaches that evil and the consequences of evil are real. People sin regardless of how hard they try not to. This fact is self-evident. All societies have laws to curb people's natural tendency to put self first. Jealousy, lying, revenge, bitterness, hate, and malice are inescapable human traits present to some degree in everyone.

Centuries of effort have failed to curb humanities proclivity to sin. The twentieth century has experienced as much, if not more, human suffering, disease, famine, major war, and threat of war, as any other time in history. Modern society is marked by the disintegration of the family, moral depravity, violent crimes, political corruption, self-centeredness, greed, and pride.

Which view of reality—Christian or New Age—is in harmony with human nature and the world as we observe it? In Geisler's words, "As man comes to know more about the true nature of reality, he discovers that the view of reality portrayed in biblical theism is remarkably similar to the nature of reality as observed."[5]

What can we conclude from all this with regard to the objective authenticity of the Christian worldview? Just this. If Christian truth-claims can be demonstrated to be factual in every area in which they can be checked out—including its analysis and description of human nature and the human condition—then we can logically and safely conclude that its spiritual truth-claims—and its answers to life's problems—are equally true. The Christian religion is God's chosen medium of revelation and the Bible its inerrant record.

Christianity Is Subjectively True

Christianity is subjectively true in three broad ways. First, it promises eternal life (1 John 5:11–13). Of course, if Christianity is true, then it is only through Jesus Christ that eternal life in heaven is attained.

Second, Christianity offers peace of mind by answering life's most perplexing questions in a relevant and believable way that corresponds to reality. It gives answers to precisely the same questions that the non-Christian world cannot answer: Who am I? Where did I come from? Why am I here? What happens to me when I die?

These questions are unanswerable by secular philosophies such as naturalism and humanism because they involve issues those worldviews don't address. Nor are they answerable by non-Christian religions because those religions do not have religious truth—they are not divine revelation. These questions can be answered only by an all-powerful, all-wise God who knows our deepest needs because He is our creator.

Finally Christianity is subjectively true because it meets human needs at their deepest level by providing something no other religion or secular worldview can provide. Being a Christian is not always easy, and God never promised that our pilgrimage though this life would be pain free. Nevertheless, Jesus takes our old sinful nature, our broken and beaten self, and replaces it with a new, spirit-filled nature that is empowered by God to resist sin and to live in obedience to Him (Rom. 6:6–7; 2 Tim. 1:7).

Jesus makes changes in the inner person. While other religions have rules and regulations to follow, Christianity has a risen Savior who promises a born-again life if we trust in Him (John 3:3). Jesus assures us that He "came that [we] might have life, and might have it abundantly" (John 10:10; see Phil. 4:5–7, 19).

Twenty centuries have passed since the resurrection of Jesus Christ. During that time, countless millions of men, women, and children have had dramatic, life-changing encounters with the risen Lord. Atheists and skeptics have become believers, marriages have been restored, life-controlling drug and alcohol addictions have been cured, damaged emotions have been healed, and broken relationships mended. As one author described it: "Christian faith displaces irrationality with meaning, anxiety with courage, hate with love, guilt with forgiveness, alienation with fellowship, impotence with dynamic, despair with hope, and pride with humility. If truth about reality includes truth about man's psychological well-being, then Christianity is true."[6]

This is powerful subjective testimony to the reality of Christianity.

Truth or Consequences

Christian apologist Edward John Carnell suggested that "death *may* be worse than life."[7] If Christianity is God's only avenue of divine revelation, if it is only through Jesus Christ that we receive eternal life in heaven, then it follows that rejecting Christianity results in eternal separation from God outside of heaven. This conclusion is not a matter of what we believe or disbelieve, understand or don't understand, or whether the statement is arrogant and exclusive or humble and compelling. Christians are making a truth-claim that is a matter of fact, not opinion. If the claim is true, common sense dictates that all other religious and secular worldviews *must* point away from truth.

If you are an unbeliever, I hope this book has challenged you to compare your existing religious or secular worldview with Christianity. I have tried to demonstrate beyond reasonable doubt that only Christianity can sustain its truth-claims by rational, objective evidence.

People constantly make excuses for not opening their hearts and minds to Christ: I don't want to be bothered by God right now—maybe later. I'm basically a good person; God will forgive me of my small sins and take me into heaven. All religions lead to God, so what difference does it make what I choose to believe?

I have repeatedly pointed out that truth is not dictated by personal opinion. Scripture teaches that we are accountable for what we do with the information about God we have (Luke 12:47–48; John 15:22; 2 Peter 2:21). Lame excuses will be seen in their true colors when we stand before Almighty God to give account of ourselves (Rev. 20:11–12; cf. Matt. 7:21–23).

The Bible clearly teaches that God does not want anyone to suffer eternal damnation (1 Tim. 2:4; 1 Peter 3:9). Yet it also teaches that people can reject God's offer of salvation only so long. We can reach a point when we step over the line, where we are alive physically but dead spiritually. Just as we can build callouses on our hands so that we no longer feel tenderness when using a pick and shovel, so we can form callouses around our hearts so that we no longer feel God's tender call. When we reach this point, there is virtually no hope of salvation.

This is a hard saying, but it's true. We can harden ourselves to God's gift of salvation to the point where we are unable to respond. In 2 Chronicles 36, King Zedekiah and the priests "continually mocked the messages of God, despised His words and scoffed at His prophets, until the wrath of the Lord arose against His people, until there was no remedy" (v. 16). In their rebellion, in their rejection of God, the king and the priests had reached a point of no return (cf. Jer. 11:11; 14:11–12; 15:1–2). We can do the same thing in our own rebellion against God.

Think about this a moment. Can you imagine anything worse than being eternally separated from God? Imagine an eternity of suffering and rejection away from the love and grace and joy and bliss of heaven. What tragedy is worse than rejecting forever the opportunity to live in a pain-free, tear-free environment where all past mistakes and sins are forgiven (Rev. 21:1–5)?

It's important that we realize that God doesn't "send" anyone to hell. We *choose* hell over heaven by willfully rejecting God's offer of salvation through Jesus Christ. Since Jesus is one in essence with God the Father, part of the triune Godhead, rejecting the Son is tantamount to rejecting the Father—a willful rejection of Jesus is the same thing as a willful rejection of God. Such an act results in eternal separation from God. Thus people enter a Christless eternity by slapping away God's extended hand of forgiveness, love, and fellowship.

In Ephesians 4:17–19 (NIV), the apostle Paul wrote:

> So I tell you this, and insist on it in the Lord, that you must no longer live as the Gentiles [unbelievers] do, in the futility of their thinking. They are darkened in their understanding and separated from the life of God because of the ignorance that is in them due *to the hardening of their hearts.* [emphasis mine]

Notice that the ignorance in them is not a lack of information about God, but a volitional hardening of their hearts against God.

Romans 1:18 helps to clarify this: "The wrath of God is being revealed from heaven against all the godlessness and wickedness of men who *suppress* the truth by their wickedness" (emphasis mine). We can't suppress truth unless we possess it or have been offered it.

What are the consequences of suppressing God's truth? The text in Romans continues: "Furthermore, since they did not think it worthwhile to *retain the knowledge* of God, he gave them over to a depraved mind. . . . Although they *know* God's righteous decree that those who do such things *deserve death*" (vv. 28, 32, emphasis mine).

People reach a point where no amount of evidence can penetrate their hardened shell of disbelief. As Jesus Himself said in the story of Lazarus, "If [people] do not listen to Moses and the Prophets [i.e., the testimony of Scripture], they will not be convinced even if someone rises from the dead" (Luke 16:31). Isn't this what Jesus did to prove that He is Lord and Savior, the holy Son of God (Rom. 1:4)? When such powerful evidence is continually rejected, as the apostle Peter said, the Lord "hold[s] the unrighteous for the day of judgment" (2 Peter 2:9).

Beware of Wolves in Sheep's Clothing

Many unbelievers think that they have attained religious truth in spite of rejecting Jesus. But again, believing in something doesn't automatically make it true. Satan perpetuates just such a deception. We are warned in Scripture that "many false prophets have gone out into the world" (1 John 4:1). These counterfeit religious leaders can sound genuine and appear to possess great spiritual knowledge, even to the point that they can "show great signs and wonders" (Matt. 24:24). But Paul warned us that "even Satan disguises himself as an angel of light" (2 Cor. 11:14, also see 2 Cor. 4:4) and cautioned us to "see to it that no one takes [us] captive through philosophy and empty deception, according to the tradition of men, according to the elementary principles of the world, rather than according to Christ" (Col. 2:8).

How do we discern the false prophet from the genuine? God provides a simple test: He "who denies that Jesus is the Christ [the divine Messiah, fully God and fully man]. . . . is the antichrist [because] he denies the Father and the Son. No one who denies the Son has the Father; whoever acknowledges the Son has the Father also" (1 John 2:22–23). John continued: "This is how you can recognize the Spirit of God: Every spirit that acknowledges that Jesus Christ has come in the flesh is from God, but every spirit that does not acknowledge Jesus is not from God. This is the spirit of the antichrist" (4:2–3).

Without exception, every religion in the world *except* Christianity rejects the biblical revelation that Jesus is the incarnate Son of God—fully God and fully human, yet one in essence with the Father and the Holy Spirit.

We are further cautioned by the apostle Paul to reject any concept of Jesus that is not taught by the apostles or any spirit not from Christ or any gospel different than Scripture (2 Cor. 11:4; 13–15). Paul writes elsewhere that, "even though we, or an angel from heaven, should preach to you a gospel contrary to that which we have preached to you, let him be accursed" (Gal. 1:8). In short, we are to reject as demonic any counterfeit concept of Jesus or any teaching about Him that is contrary to Scripture.

The Challenge

Christianity is truth; it's reality. Yet many people won't investigate it. Why? Most unbelievers do not understand what Christianity is about. They *hear* that it's exclusive and narrow-minded—as if this somehow invalidates truth. But whether or not Christianity is exclusive and narrow-minded has nothing to do with whether or not it's true. The issue is truth.

In a sense, Christians are exclusive and narrow-minded. Can you see why? Christians possess the truth, and they want to share this good news with everyone. Jesus said, "I am the way and the truth and the life. No one comes to the Father except through me" (John 14:6). If God sets such a standard, is it exclusive and narrow-minded to condemn other worldviews and to try to get people to turn their lives over to Jesus Christ? Indeed, it would be unjust to do otherwise.

The human race is clearly in rebellion against God. The apostle Paul recorded in Scripture nearly two thousand years ago what to expect as the final chapter of life on earth comes to a close. Judge for yourself if this is not an apt description of modern society living under the umbrellas of secular humanism and postmodernism:

> But mark this: There will be terrible times in the last days. People will be lovers of themselves, lovers of money, boastful, proud, abusive, disobedient to their parents, ungrateful, unholy, without love, unforgiving, slanderous, without self-control, brutal, not lovers of the good, treacherous, rash, conceited, lovers of pleasure rather than lovers of God—having a form of godliness but denying its power. Have nothing to do with them. . . . For the time will come when men will not put up with sound doctrine. Instead, to suit their own desires, they will gather around them a great number of teachers to say what their itching ears want to hear. They will turn their ears away from the truth and turn aside to myths. *(2 Tim. 3:1–5; 4:3–4, NIV)*

It is precisely because Christianity so accurately describes and understands the human condition that it can prescribe the medicine needed for a cure. This "medicine" is Jesus Christ.

You see, Christianity is not a religion, not in the sense of people seeking God through rituals, meditations, incantations, and good works. Rather Christianity is a relationship. It is a relationship of love with God made possible because Jesus Christ died on the cross to be the Savior of the world (1 John 2:2). Salvation is a free gift from God (Eph. 2:8–9). Our only responsibility is to accept it on God's terms.

If Jesus is who He claims to be and who His disciples say He is—God incarnate, the Savior of the world—this is not merely an academic matter. It is not a question of intellectual choice or preference. Rather the decision to receive or reject Jesus is the most important decision in the world. It's literally a matter of life and death.

If you are an unbeliever, won't you honestly investigate Christianity? Eternity is forever. Why take a chance? Check out the facts. Pray to God that He will open your heart and mind to the truth of Jesus Christ. A new and exciting life waits to be discovered. As Jesus said, "Then you will know the truth, and the truth will set you free" (John 8:32).

Notes

Chapter One:
The World We Live In

1. David F. Wells, *No Place for Truth: Or Whatever Happened to Evangelical Theology?* (Grand Rapids: Eerdmans, 1993), 263.
2. D. A. Carson, "Christian Witness in an Age of Pluralism," in *God and Culture: Essays in Honor of Carl F. H. Henry,* ed. D. A. Carson and John D. Woodbridge (Grand Rapids: Eerdmans, 1993), 44.
3. Wells, *No Place for Truth,* 269–79.
4. Ibid., 40.
5. Norman L. Geisler and William D. Watkins, *Worlds Apart: A Handbook on World Views* (Grand Rapids: Baker, 1989), 59.
6. Alister McGrath, *A Passion for Truth: The Intellectual Coherence of Evangelism* (Downers Grove, Ill.: InterVarsity Press, 1996), chap. 5. This chapter provides a good analysis of the tension between religious pluralism (and its political agenda) and orthodox evangelism.
7. Ibid., 211.
8. Carson, *God and Culture,* 39.
9. Ibid.
10. Ibid., 34, 36.
11. Eccl. 3:11; Acts 14:17; 17:24–27; Rom. 1:19–20.
12. Edith Hamilton, *Mythology: Timeless Tales of God and Heroes* (New York: New American Library of World Literature, 1963), 27.

13. Geisler and Watkins, *Worlds Apart,* 218.
14. Ibid., 241, 245.
15. George Barna, *The Barna Report 1992–1993: An Annual Survey of Life-styles, Values, and Religious Views* (Ventura, Calif.: Regal, 1992), 44, 156.
16. Some pantheists accept the existence of other deities. However, their philosophical view of ultimate reality includes a concept of God as described here and in chapter eight.

Chapter Two:
Firming the Foundation of Truth

1. Gordon H. Clark, *Logic* (Jefferson, Md.: Trinity Foundation, 1988), 150–51.
2. For further reading in this area I recommend two books: Dennis McCallum, *The Death of Truth* (Minneapolis: Bethany House, 1996) and James W. Sire, *Why Should Anyone Believe Anything at All?* (Downers Grove, Ill.: InterVarsity Press, 1994).
3. Sire, *Why Should Anyone Believe Anything At All?* 79.
4. Ibid., 221.
5. J. P. Moreland, *Christianity and the Nature of Science: A Philosophical Investigation* (Grand Rapids: Baker, 1989), 118.
6. Norman L. Geisler and Ronald M. Brooks, *Come, Let Us Reason Together: An Introduction to Logical Thinking* (Grand Rapids: Baker, 1990), 16.
7. Norman L. Geisler and Ronald M. Brooks, *When Skeptics Ask: A Handbook on Christian Evidences* (Wheaton, Ill.: Victor, 1990), 272.
8. Also see Walter R. Martin, *The Kingdom of the Cults,* 123–25.
9. Mark M. Hanna, *Crucial Questions in Apologetics* (Grand Rapids: Baker, 1981), 115.

Chapter Three:
Is Truth Relatively True or Absolutely True?

1. Geisler and Brooks, *Come, Let Us Reason Together,* 255.
2. Barna, *The Barna Report 1992–1993,* 50.
3. Ibid., 76.
4. Ibid., 44.
5. See C. S. Lewis, *The Abolition of Man: How Education Develops Man's Sense of Morality* (New York: Macmillan, 1955).
6. Francis J. Beckwith, *Politically Correct Death: Answering Arguments for Abortion Rights* (Grand Rapids: Baker, 1993), 24.

7. Ibid.
8. Norman L. Geisler, "Any Absolutes? Absolutely!" *Christian Research Journal* (summer 1995), 14–15. This is an excellent summary of the arguments for absolute ethics from the perspective of the Christian worldview.
9. Geisler and Watkins, *Worlds Apart,* 174.

Chapter Four:
A World of My Own

1. Francis A. Schaeffer, *The God Who Is There: Speaking Historic Christianity into the Twentieth Century* (Downers Grove, Ill.: InterVarsity Press, 1968), 143.
2. Ronald H. Nash, *Worldviews in Conflict: Choosing Christianity in a World of Ideas* (Grand Rapids: Zondervan, 1992), 53.
3. Geisler and Watkins, *Worlds Apart,* 11.
4. Ibid., 14.
5. James W. Sire, *The Universe Next Door: A Basic World View Catalog* (Downers Grove, Ill.: InterVarsity Press, 1988), 17.
6. Alister E. McGrath, *Intellectuals Don't Need God & Other Modern Myths* (Grand Rapids: Zondervan, 1993), 162.
7. Quoted in Josh McDowell, *More Evidence That Demands a Verdict: Historical Evidences for the Christian Scriptures,* rev. ed. (San Bernardino, Calif.: Here's Life Publishers, 1981), 7.
8. Geisler and Watkins, *Worlds Apart,* 12.
9. Ronald H. Nash, *Faith & Reason: Searching for a Rational Faith* (Grand Rapids: Zondervan, 1988), 30.
10. Garry Friesen with J. Robin Maxson, *Decision Making & the Will of God: A Biblical Alternative to the Traditional View* (Portland, Ore.: Multnomah, 1980). This is a good, thought-provoking book on the role of personal choice in discerning and living out God's will for believers.

Chapter Five:
Testing Truth-Claims for Truth

1. Some truth can be wholly subjective in nature. This is especially the case in the area of aesthetics. For example, my favorite color is green. This is my personal opinion and is not verifiable by outside (objective) criteria. That the color green is my favorite color is true for me. Likewise, I have favorite paintings, vacation spots, movies, and

books—all of them not subject to objective truth-testing. Yet in that I believe they represent the best in their respective categories, they are *true* to me.

2. Walter Martin, *The New Cults* (Ventura, Calif.: Regal, 1980), 17–18.
3. Sire, *Why Should Anyone Believe Anything at All?* 65–66.
4. Norman Geisler, *Christian Apologetics* (Grand Rapids: Baker, 1987), chap. 6.
5. Ibid., 113.
6. Ibid., 115.
7. Gary R. Habermas and Terry L. Miethe, *Why Believe? God Exists!* (Joplin, Mo.: College Press, 1993), 45.
8. McGrath, *Intellectuals Don't Need God,* 147.
9. Geisler, *Christian Apologetics*, 44.
10. Geisler and Brooks, *When Skeptics Ask,* 267.
11. Norman L. Geisler, *Signs and Wonders* (Wheaton, Ill.: Tyndale House, 1984), 99.
12. William James, *The Varieties of Religious Experiences: A Study in Human Nature* (New York: Macmillan, 1961), 337.
13. Harman J. Eckelmann, "An Evidential Approach to Biblical Christianity," in *Evidence for Faith: Deciding the God Question,* ed. John Warwick Montgomery (Dallas: Probe Books, 1991), 27.
14. J. P. Moreland, *Scaling the Secular City: A Defense of Christianity* (Grand Rapids: Baker, 1991), 232.
15. Ibid.
16. Wells, *No Place for Truth,* 173.
17. Ibid., 184.
18. C. S. Lewis, *God in the Dock: Essays on Theology and Ethics* (Grand Rapids: Eerdmans, 1994), 141.
19. James, *The Varieties of Religious Experiences,* 150.
20. Ibid.
21. Ibid., 73.
22. Moreland, *Scaling the Secular City,* 238–39.
23. John Warwick Montgomery, *The Shape of the Past: A Christian Response to Secular Philosophies of History* (Minneapolis: Bethany House, 1975), 265.

Chapter Six:
The Whole Truth and Nothing but the Truth

1. Geisler and Brooks, *Come, Let Us Reason,* 138–40.
2. Montgomery, "The Jury Returns: A Juridical Defense of Christianity," in *Evidence for Faith,* 332–33.

3. Nash, *Faith & Reason*, 65.

4. Norman Geisler and Winfried Corduan, *Philosophy of Religion*, 2nd ed. (Grand Rapids: Baker, 1993), 88.

5. Simon Greenleaf, *The Testimony of the Evangelists: The Gospels Examined by the Rules of Evidence Administered in Courts of Justice* (Grand Rapids, Mich.: Kregel Publications, 1995), 28.

6. Ibid., 29.

7. Ibid.

8. Ibid., 40–41.

9. Edward John Carnell, *An Introduction to Christian Apologetics: A Philosophic Defense of the Trinitarian-Theistic Faith* (Grand Rapids: Eerdmans, 1952), 113.

10. Nash, *Faith & Reason*, 118.

11. Arthur Beiser and editors of Time Life Books, *Life Nature Library: The Earth* (New York: Time Life Books, 1970), 32.

12. Montgomery, *The Shape of the Past*, 229.

13. Montgomery, *Evidence for Faith*, 332.

14. Greenleaf, *The Testimony of the Evangelists*, 32.

15. Habermas and Miethe, *Why Believe?* 241.

16. Two excellent books on the historical reliability of Scripture are: F. F. Bruce, *The New Testament Documents: Are They Reliable?* (Downers Grove, Ill.: InterVarsity Press, 5th ed., 1984) and John Warwick Montgomery, *History and Christianity* (San Bernardino, Calif.: Here's Life Publishers, 1983).

17. Many books have been written that record details of fulfilled Old Testament prophecy. Good introductory studies include Josh McDowell, *Evidence That Demands a Verdict*, chapters 9 and 11, and John Warwick Montgomery, ed., *Evidence for Faith*, chapter 4.

18. John Ankerberg, John Weldon, and Walter C. Kaiser Jr., *The Case for Jesus the Messiah: Incredible Prophecies that Prove God Exists* (Eugene, Ore.: Harvest House, 1989).

Chapter Seven:
Christianity: God Is God

1. Dan Story, *Defending Your Faith: Reliable Answers for a New Generation of Seekers and Skeptics* (Grand Rapids: Kregel, 1997).

2. Nelson Glueck, *Rivers in the Desert* (Philadelphia: Jewish Publications Society of America, 1969), 31.

Chapter Eight:
Pantheism: All Is God

1. For a superb study of heresies, see Harold O. J. Brown, *Heresies: The Image of Christ in the Mirror of Heresy and Orthodoxy from the Apostles to the Present* (Garden City, N.Y.: Doubleday, 1984), 2–3.
2. This includes many who should know better. Even many Christian leaders are entertaining New Age concepts. See Hank Hanegraaff, *Christianity in Crisis* (Eugene, Ore.: Harvest House, 1993) and Michael Horton, ed., *The Agony of Deceit: What Some TV Preachers Are Really Teaching* (Chicago: Moody, 1990).
3. Geisler and Brooks, *When Skeptics Ask,* 41.
4. Sire, *The Universe Next Door,* 139.
5. For further study, see Geisler and Watkins, *Worlds Apart*; Geisler, *Christian Apologetics,* chap. 10; and Sire, *The Universe Next Door.*
6. Sire, *The Universe Next Door,* 139.
7. Ibid., 140.
8. Geisler, *Christian Apologetics,* 185.
9. Sire, *The Universe Next Door,* 142.
10. Geisler, *Christian Apologetics,* 185.
11. Dennis McCallum, *The Death of Truth* (Minneapolis: Bethany House, 1996), 205.
12. Sire, *The Universe Next Door,* 165.
13. Ibid., 172.
14. Ibid., 203–4.
15. Geisler, *Christian Apologetics,* 187.
16. Ibid., 189.
17. Sire, *The Universe Next Door,* 201.

Chapter Nine:
What About Other Religions?

1. Wells, *No Place for Truth,* 262.
2. Josh McDowell and John Gilchrist, *The Islam Debate* (San Bernardino, Calif.: Here's Life Publishers, 1983), 35.
3. McCallum, *The Death of Truth,* 207.
4. Martin, *The New Cults,* 21.
5. Quoted in Martin, *The Kingdom of the Cults,* 11.
6. Martin, *The New Cults,* 16.
7. James W. Sire, *Scripture Twisting: 20 Ways the Cults Misread the Bible* (Downers Grove, Ill.: InterVarsity Press, 1980), 21.
8. Martin, *The Kingdom of the Cults,* 11.

9. Ibid., 18.
10. Mary Baker Eddy, *Science and Health with Key to the Scriptures* (Boston: Published by the Trustees under the Will of Mary Baker G. Eddy, 1934), 579.
11. Ibid., 581.
12. Ibid.
13. Ibid., 584.
14. Ibid., 586.
15. Ibid., 589.
16. Ibid., 592.
17. Sire, *Scripture Twisting*, 12.
18. Eddy, *Science and Health,* 109.
19. Walter Martin, *The Maze of Mormonism* (Ventura, Calif.: Regal Books, 1985), 163.
20. Ibid., 170–94.

Chapter Ten:
Naturalism: There Is No God

1. Nash, *Faith & Reason,* 47–48.
2. Quoted in Sire, *The Universe Next Door,* 63.
3. For evidence of the existence of God, see Habermas and Miethe, *Why Believe? God Exists!* and Peter Kreeft and Ronald K. Tacelli, *Handbook of Christian Apologetics* (Downers Grove, Ill.: InterVarsity Press, 1994), chap. 3.
4. Moreland, *Christianity and the Nature of Science,* 107.
5. Ibid., 104.
6. Ibid., 107.
7. Ibid.
8. Phillip E. Johnson, *Reason in the Balance: The Case Against Naturalism in Science, Law & Education* (Downers Grove, Ill.: InterVarsity Press), 100.
9. Quoted in Habermas and Miethe, *Why Believe? God Exists!* 107.
10. Larry Laudan, *Progress and Its Problems: Toward a Theory of Scientific Growth* (Berkeley, Calif.: Univ. of Calif. Press, 1977).
11. Montgomery, *The Shape of the Past,* 138–39. Also see, Bruce, *New Testament Documents.*
12. Michael J. Wilkins and J. P. Moreland, *Jesus Under Fire* (Grand Rapids: Zondervan, 1995), 198.
13. Two books on this subject are: Roy Abraham Varghese, ed., *The Intellectuals Speak Out About God* (Dallas: Lewis & Stanley, 1984) and Luther D. Sunderland, *Darwin's Enigma: Fossils & Other Problems* (Santee, Calif.: Master Book, 1984).

14. Sunderland, *Darwin's Enigma,* 53–62.
15. Moreland, *Christianity and the Nature of Science,* 52–53.

Chapter Eleven:
Secular Humanism: Man Is God

1. Sire, *The Universe Next Door,* 74.
2. Harold J. Berry, *Secular Humanism* (Lincoln, Neb.: Back to the Bible, 1990), 7.
3. Cited in Steve Hallman, "Christianity and Humanism: A Study in Contrasts," *AFA Journal* (March 1991), 6.
4. Francis A. Schaeffer, *A Christian Manifesto* (Westchester, Ill.: Crossway Books, 1986), 24.
5. Ibid., 48–49.
6. Joseph P. Gudel, "'That Which Is Unnatural': Homosexuality in Society, the Church, and Scripture," *Christian Research Journal* (winter 1993), 10.
7. Quoted in Ibid.
8. Ibid., 11.
9. Schaeffer, *A Christian Manifesto,* 29–30.
10. Harvey Cox, *The Secular City* (New York: Macmillan, 1965) quoted in Hallman, "Christianity and Humanism: A Study in Contrasts," 7.
11. Ibid., 15.
12. Ibid., 8.
13. Harold Lindsell, *The Bible in the Balance* (Grand Rapids: Zondervan, 1979), 277. Quotes by Dr. Lindsell from Paul Tournier, *The Whole Person in a Broken World* (New York: Harper & Row, 1977), 4.
14. Peter Gay, *The Enlightenment: An Interpretation: The Rise of Modern Paganism* (New York: Norton, 1966), 280.
15. Ibid., 269–70.
16. Ibid., 275–76.
17. Ibid., 314.
18. Gay, *The Enlightenment: An Interpretation,* is an excellent study of the Enlightenment for readers interested in a full academic treatment. A book designed for a popular readership is Harold Lindsell, *The New Paganism* (San Francisco, Calif.: Harper & Row, 1987).
19. Goeffrey Bruun, *The Enlightened Despots* (New York: Henry Holt, 1922), 9.
20. Ernest Cassierer, *The Philosophy of the Enlightenment,* trans. Fritz C. A. Koelin & James Pettegrove (Boston: Beacon, 1965), 134.
21. James C. Livingston, *Modern Christian Thought From the Enlightenment to Vatican II* (New York: Macmillan, 1971), 2.

22. Ibid., 222.
23. Langdon Gilkey, *Religion and the Scientific Future: Reflections on Myth, Science, and Theology* (Macon, Ga.: Mercer Univ., 1981), 8.
24. Story, *Defending Your Faith.*
25. Robert A. Morey, *The New Atheism and the Erosion of Freedom* (Minneapolis: Presbyterian and Reformed Publishing, 1986), 148–49.
26. Sir Fred Catherwood, "The Christian and Politics" in *God and Culture,* ed. D. A. Carson and John D. Woodbridge, 208.
27. Ibid., 204.
28. David Barton, *The Myth of Separation: What Is the Correct Relationship between Church and State* (Aledo, Tex.: WallBuilder, 1992), 209–16. These pages contain useful graphs showing various areas of moral decline between the years 1950 and 1990.
29. Wells, *No Place for Truth,* 171.
30. Hallman, "Christianity and Humanism," 17.
31. Williston Walker et al., *A History of the Christian Church,* 4th ed. (New York: Scribner's, 1985), 596–97.
32. Earle E. Cairns, *Christianity Through the Centuries: A History of the Christian Church* (Grand Rapids: Zondervan, 1981), 382.
33. R. A. Torrey, *The Power of Prayer and the Prayer of Power* (Grand Rapids: Zondervan, 1971), 189.
34. Catherwood, "The Christian and Politics," 205.
35. Wells, *No Place for Truth,* 161–66, 198–201. In these pages, David Wells gives a good analysis of the "importance of television in the shaping of the American Character today."
36. Schaeffer, *A Christian Manifesto,* 66.
37. Steve Hallman, "Christianity and Humanism," 18–19.

Chapter Twelve:
Postmodernism: God Is Whomever

1. William Lane Craig, "Politically Incorrect Salvation," in *Christian Apologetics in the Postmodern World,* ed. Timothy R. Phillips and Dennis L. Okholm (Downers Grove, Ill.: InterVarsity Press, 1995), 81.
2. Dennis McCallum, *The Death of Truth* (Minneapolis: Bethany House, 1996).
3. Ibid., 11–13.
4. McGrath, *A Passion for Truth,* 164.
5. Over the last few years, an increasing number of books have been published that deal specifically with postmodernism. Two books, taken together, which provide a good introductory study of postmodernism are: Dennis McCallum, ed., *The Death of Truth* and

William D. Watkins, *The New Absolutes*, both published by Bethany House Publishers.

6. McGrath, *A Passion for Truth*, 186.
7. Jim Leffel, "Our New Challenge: Postmodernism," in *The Death of Truth*, 31.
8. Ibid., 40.
9. Jim Leffel, "Postmodernism and 'The Myth of Progress': Two Visions," in *The Death of Truth*, 49.
10. Phillips and Okholm, *Christian Apologetics in the Postmodern World*, 14.
11. Ibid.
12. McGrath, *A Passion for Truth*, 191–92.
13. Ibid., 192.
14. Leffel, "Postmodernism and 'The Myth of Progress'" in *The Death of Truth*, 50.
15. Ibid.
16. Ibid., 51.
17. Ibid.
18. McCallum, "Evangelical Imperatives," in *The Death of Truth*, 245.
19. McGrath, *A Passion for Truth*, 190.
20. Watkins, *The New Absolutes* (Minneapolis: Bethany House, 1996), 36.
21. Ibid., 38.
22. Ibid., 39.
23. Ibid., 41.
24. McCallum, "Evangelical Imperatives," in *The Death of Truth*, 245.
25. The problem of evil is atheism's *only* so-called proof that God doesn't exist. All other arguments against God's existence are actually arguments against evidence that He *does* exist. For example, evolution is not a direct attack against God's existence. Rather it's an argument against creationism—which is proof that God does exist. Peter Kreeft and Ronald Tacelli point this out in their *Handbook of Christian Apologetics* (Downers Grove, Ill.: InterVarsity Press, 1994): "There are many proofs or apparent proofs of theism . . . but there is only one argument that even claims to prove there is no God [i.e., problem of evil]. There are many other arguments against theism, but none of them amounts to a proof or demonstration. For instance, there are objections to all the arguments *for* theism, but even if they are successful, these objections only refute the arguments as invalid and inconclusive. They do not thereby *dis*prove God's existence" (p. 122).
26. Miethe and Habermas, *Why Believe? God Exists!* 201.
27. Ibid.

28. Dennis Hollinger, "The Church As Apologetic: A Sociology of Knowledge Perspective," in *Christian Apologetics in the Postmodern World,* 187.

29. Phillips and Okholm, *Christian Apologetics in the Postmodern World,* 21–22.

30. Hollinger, in *Christian Apologetics in the Postmodern World,* 186.

Chapter Thirteen:
"Death *May* Be Worse than Life"

1. James, *The Varieties of Religious Experiences,* 123.

2. Ibid., 123–24.

3. Edward John Carnell, *A Philosophy of the Christian Religion* (Grand Rapids: Eerdmans, 1952), 19.

4. Geisler and Corduan, *Philosophy of Religion,* 2nd ed., 72.

5. Norman L. Geisler, *The Roots of Evil,* 2nd ed. (Dallas: Probe Books, 1989), 79–80.

6. Gordon R. Lewis, *Testing Christianity's Truth Claims: Approaches to Christian Apologetics* (Chicago: Moody, 1976), 251.

7. Carnell, *A Philosophy of the Christian Religion,* 19.

DEFENDING YOUR FAITH

Reliable Answers for a New Generation of Seekers and Skeptics

by Dan Story

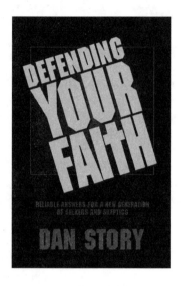

How do I know that God exists?
Can I trust the Bible?
Why is there evil and suffering in the world?
Is God an environmentalist?
Are the Bible and science in conflict?

Whether you want to grow in your understanding of truth or need trustworthy responses to the questions of friends, Dan Story has the answers.

This book is designed to help Christians see that Christianity is reasonable and intelligent faith grounded on objective, verifiable evidence. It will also enable readers to share these answers with family, friends, and coworkers who have questions about Christianity.

"It is apologetics that needs no apology."   —R. C. Sproul

ISBN 0-8254-3675-3   **242 pp.**